COMPUTER EFFECTIVENESS

Computer

INFORMATION RESOURCES PRESS

WASHINGTON, D.C.   1979

C. WARREN AXELROD

Effectiveness

Bridging the
Management/Technology Gap

Available from
Information Resources Press
2100 M Street, N.W.
Washington, D.C. 20037

Library of Congress Catalog Card Number 79-53113

ISBN 0–87815–028–5

CONTENTS

v

FOREWORD

For some time now, the computer performance evaluation community has been trying to bridge the gap between its own techniques and data-processing management. *Computer Effectiveness* significantly reduces that gap by defining computer system effectiveness in terms a manager can understand and by creating an analytical framework that is both intelligible and implementable. *Computer Effectiveness* is an important book that integrates the concept of controlling data-processing value into the framework of data-processing management.

Most books concerned with *computer performance evaluation* and *computer systems measurement* are technique-oriented; they deal with bits and pieces of the data-processing management puzzle but never come to grips with the real problem of how to make data processing more productive. *Computer Effectiveness* does not attempt to tell you how to manage an installation or what to measure and report to management. It does, however, contain clear definitions of what data-processing management should strive for and intelligent discussions of techniques that are central to maximizing the value produced by a data-processing system. *Computer Effectiveness* brings together a number of performance-related management decision areas that have never before been integrated in a single framework. Budgeting, pricing, scheduling, sequencing, and value considerations are first melded into organizational models and information decision and control models and then into procedures for allocating computer resources (from long-range planning to short-term operational scheduling). This is achieved through the book's unique value function concept that links planning and control decisions over time. *Computer Effectiveness* clearly explains how each decision area affects performance and how the different areas are related to one another. Dr. Axelrod's straightforward and readable prose relies only minimally on mathematics.

Computer Effectiveness is a significant intellectual contribution that should go far in redirecting the thoughts and activities of data-processing managers, researchers, and technicians. Spanning economics, operations research, management science, and general management, the book will appeal to a wide readership. It is hoped that the audience will, in its turn, contribute to improving our ability to manage, control, and make more effective the computer systems that so dominate our economy and influence our lives.

PHILIP J. KIVIAT

PREFACE

Prior to the 1970s, control of the computer was largely the domain of the technologist. The activities within the walls of the computer center generally were not understood, much less controlled, by management. As more and more organization resources were poured into data processing and a greater dependency on computers evolved, general management asked: "What are we getting for our money?" The data-processing manager, in turn, would point to high equipment utilizations, numerous applications processed, and increased demands from users. To justify additional equipment, he also would emphasize the inevitable saturation of present equipment, the additional applications that could be processed on new equipment, and the risk of not meeting deadlines and other processing requirements with existing hardware. His presentations invariably included terms such as CPU (central processing unit) utilization and MIPS (millions of instructions processed per second)—terms which are meaningless or, worse, misleading to a management concerned primarily with maintaining or increasing profits.

A means of evaluating the effectiveness of computer resources has been needed to enable measurement of the net value of the work done. With more data-processing (DP) managers advancing to the ranks of general management and with general management becoming more familiar with computers, the question of what the value of computing might be is asked much more frequently and with greater understanding. The answer, however, is illusive, partly due to the lack of a useful framework for evaluating computer effectiveness.

Recently, a number of books and articles have stressed the need for communication and understanding between management and data processing. Some provide basic evaluation techniques, such as specific worksheets, to be used by the DP manager; others attempt to teach non-DP management about computers. Although these efforts are praiseworthy, they are not entirely satisfactory, because neither party gains adequate knowledge of the other's field to make good decisions. To counteract this problem, the introduction of an intermediary—an ombudsman well versed in "computerese" and business management—has been recommended to bring together managers and technologists in a productive environment. This approach implies that an interpreter will resolve the problem that presumably arose from lack of communication. Semantic and technical links are important, but an essential ingredient is still missing. The liaison should not provide merely a channel for communication, but should be based on a workable analytical structure so that requirements for computer effectiveness of both general and data-processing management can be expressed in a common language and solutions can be mutually understood.

In this book, the bridging role is called the "central control." The staffing requirements of this function will vary in level and capability from one organization to the next, depending on factors such as the size and importance of the computer function. "Information resource manager," "time-sharing administrator," "DP systems controller," and "computer resource manager" will become pervasive titles within the central control area. Except for cosmetic differences, the basic central control function will be common to practically all organizations with significant computing needs and will follow the formulation developed in the first part of this book.

In Chapter 3, an analysis is presented of how demand affects turnaround for an internal system and how turnaround influences demand—a vicious or virtuous circle, depending on the stability of the system. This is an important, but heretofore ignored, problem.

Presuming the existence of a central controlling function for computer resources, the problem arises as to what tools are available to serve this function. In Part II of this book, an analytical structure and a set of tools are proposed, based on a new perspective. The concept of controlling user demand is practically unheard of in the DP field, but in Chapter 6, "macrosequencing," whereby both the level and pattern of demand can be manipulated, is introduced; in order to tie together demand and the computer operation, a new concept, a value function that varies dynamically with service level, also is presented. This powerful vehicle, called a "value hill" in its simplified form, provides the basis for a series of possibilities for computer evaluation, as illustrated in Chapter 8.

Because the content of this book links management and technology, it has greatest appeal to the technically sophisticated manager and the management-oriented researcher. The former category includes general management, data-processing management, electronic data-processing (EDP) auditors, DP administrators, management consultants, practicing management scientists, and students of business. The latter category includes operations researchers, economists, and computer scientists. The manager will acquire knowledge of concepts that will clarify his approach to computer evaluation and facilitate both the analysis of situations and the presentation of results. The researcher will gain new insights into the meaning of computer resource allocation and should be guided to many exciting areas of fruitful research and development.

Many of the concepts expressed in this book originally were described in a thesis titled "The Allocation of Computing Resources in Organizations with Semi-Autonomous Users," prepared for Cornell University. I wish to acknowledge the assistance of Warren Hausman, James Kinard, Howard Morgan, Seymour Smidt, and Bernell Stone in the development of the original work, to express my appreciation to Susan Heylman and Gene Allen at Information Resources Press for their valued editorial contributions, and to thank the many others who provided suggestions and opportunities to extend and improve on the basic ideas.

Great Neck, N.Y.   C. WARREN AXELROD

PART I

1
INTRODUCTION

The "cost per computation" for electronic digital computers, which has dropped dramatically over the past two decades,[1] continues to fall as technological breakthroughs are made. Progress in electronics and communications engineering has produced innovative computing capabilities such as time-sharing, stand-alone minicomputers, and systems with distributed intelligence, providing users with previously unavailable choices for meeting their computational needs. Software advances, such as data-base management systems, simulation languages, and high-level languages for data manipulation, have resulted in more efficient use of hardware and have made available to users new types of services and facilities. Performance measurement techniques have enabled systems experts to evaluate and improve upon the efficiency of computer hardware, networks, software, and applications programs. Sophisticated scheduling schemes also have led to improvements in computer throughput by rearranging the order in which jobs are processed and optimizing the mix of concurrent jobs in multiprogramming systems.

The aforementioned approaches pertain to the efficiency of computer operations, where "Efficiency is concerned with doing things right."[2] Relatively little attention has been given to the effective use of computer resources, where "Effectiveness is doing the right things."[3]

[1]W. F. Sharpe. *The Economics of Computers.* New York, Columbia University Press, 1969, p. 323.
[2]P. F. Drucker. *Management: Tasks, Responsibilities, Practices.* New York, Harper and Row, 1974, p. 45.
[3]*Ibid.* See also R. G. Canning, ed., "Are We Doing the Right Things?"; "Are We

3

All the computer systems referred to in the following chapters will be assumed to operate with equivalent efficiency. Explicit consideration of the efficiency of computer systems is not included here but can be found in the abundant and rapidly growing literature on computer performance measurement and evaluation,[4] software and hardware selection,[5] and software development and implementation.[6]

In this book, the meaning of effectiveness with respect to the use of computers will be explored, and the methods of allocating computer resources to achieve increased net value from the work done by those resources will be developed.

CONGESTION IN ECONOMIC SYSTEMS

The problem of congestion arises whenever a service facility is unable to accommodate all customers immediately upon their arrival, in which case those customers who wait for service form a queue. Neither the service facility nor the queue must exhibit any clearly recognizable form. For example, a highway provides travelers with the means to transport their vehicles from one place to another—but this is not an actively given service. A queue may be readily discernible to observers, as in the case of customers waiting at a supermarket checkout counter, or it may be invisible, as when persons attempt to telephone someone whose line is busy.

Even when the queue is visible, its physical embodiment may represent only a fraction of those desiring service. For example, customers observing a line may decide not to join the queue (this is termed "balking") but to return subsequently or not at all, depending on how much they need the service. If the customer is familiar with the queueing characteristics of a particular service establishment, he might adjust his arrival time accordingly. This can be accomplished without actually observing the line itself, as, for example, when one goes to a

Doing Things Right?''; and ''Do We Have the Right Resources?''; *EDP Analyzer*, 13(5):1–12, May 1975; *13*(6):1–12; June 1975; and *13*(7):1–12, July 1975, respectively. which highlight the difference between efficiency and effectiveness in data processing.
[4]See, for example, V. K. Sahney and J. L. May, *Scheduling Computer Operations*, Computer and Information Systems Monograph Series No. 6, Norcross, Ga., American Institute of Industrial Engineers, 1972, Chapter 4.
[5]E. O. Joslin, *Computer Selection*, Fairfax Station, Va., Technology Press, 1977, provides information on equipment evaluation.
[6]W. J. Ridge and L. E. Johnson. *Effective Management of Computer Software*. Homewood, Ill., Dow Jones–Irwin, 1973.

restaurant earlier or later than the accustomed mealtime or visits a resort off-season. People tend to modify their demand for service on the basis of both the time at which the service is most desirable and the level of congestion at the service facility that could cause them delay.

In the following chapters, the effects of congestion in computer systems on the behavior of users and on the effectiveness of computers will be examined.

BACKGROUND

Many researchers and practitioners have been working toward improving the allocation of economic goods to attain higher productivity per dollar of resource. There is a growing realization, partly due to the recessions of the early and middle 1970s, that scarce and costly resources must be used as cost-effectively as possible. At the same time, computers, entering into wide business, government, and academic use, have become more visible to general management and to administrators, who are concerned with ensuring that the work done by computers warrants their expense. The response of technologists to the need for cost-effectiveness has been to try to squeeze more work units from a given piece of equipment. Economists have considered budgeting, pricing, and service priority techniques as a means of inducing appropriate computer usage. Operations researchers have emphasized scheduling of jobs to increase throughput, reduce waiting times, and promote efficient use of computer equipment. Management specialists have attempted to standardize procedures, to introduce interpersonal communications devices, and to rearrange organizational structures for improved computer operations and applications development and implementation. Although each approach contributes to an understanding of what constitutes effective computer usage and how it can be achieved, none considers the whole spectrum.

AN INTEGRATED APPROACH

To present a broader perspective on, and a more complete treatment of, computers and their use, concepts and methodologies have been drawn from a wide range of disciplines, including economics, organizational behavior, systems analysis, control engineering, management science, and operations research.[7]

---

[7]Management science and operations research often are considered to be synonymous;

Economists have examined the economic implications of congestion for systems ranging from entire national (or even world) economies to specific operations within an organization. Aroaz and Malmgren suggest some applications of queueing theory with respect to congestion situations in the workings of an economy.[8] These arise, for example, from fluctuations and imbalances in supply and demand, which lead to queues on the demand side or idle capacity of the supply mechanism.

The design and development of public transportation systems also require consideration of congestion. Vickrey evaluates the costs and benefits of investments in highways under various traffic and congestion conditions and examines the effects of congestion pricing, such as tolls.[9] He also has explored the effects of various fare policies on congestion in a city subway system.[10] To relieve congestion at airports, the levying of charges on aircraft has been suggested, based on the delays each airplane causes others wishing to land.[11]

Within business, public, and academic organizations, there are many situations to which queueing analysis can be applied. An early article by Brigham examined the problem of congestion in the context of an aircraft factory.[12] Operations research literature is replete with job-shop scheduling[13] and machine-sequencing analyses. Increasingly, queueing in computer systems, whether batch,[14] real-time,[15] or distributed networks,[16] is receiving attention.

---

however, there is a difference, in that operations research deals with the workings of all types of operations, and management science deals with the application of scientific methods to management.

[8]A. B. Aroaz and H. B. Malmgren. "Congestion and Idle Capacity in an Economy." *Review of Economic Studies, 28*:202–211, June 1961.

[9]W. S. Vickrey. "Congestion Theory and Transport Investment." *American Economic Review, 59*:251–260, May 1969.

[10]W. S. Vickrey. "A Proposal for Revising New York's Subway Fare Structure." *Journal of the Operations Research Society of America, 3*:38–68, February 1955.

[11]R. D. Eckert. *Airports and Congestion: A Problem of Misplaced Subsidies.* Washington, D.C., American Enterprise Institute for Public Policy Research, 1972.

[12]G. Brigham. "On a Congestion Problem in an Aircraft Factory." *Journal of the Operations Research Society of America, 3*:412–428, November 1955.

[13]*Computer and Job-Shop Scheduling Theory*, edited by E. G. Coffman, Jr., New York, John Wiley and Sons, 1976, examines deterministic scheduling models, particularly as they apply to computer and job-shop environments.

[14]*Ibid.*

[15]C. W. Axelrod. "Swapping Response Time for Less Switch Capacity." *Data Communications, 6*:59–64, December 1977.

[16]See L. Kleinrock, *Queueing Systems, Volume 2: Computer Applications*, New York, John Wiley and Sons, 1976, for the application of queueing theory to batch, time-sharing, and network systems.

In an economic system, a trade-off usually must be made between the level of congestion and idle capacity, since larger capacity in the service facility results in less congestion, but more unused time, for a given scheduling algorithm and arrival rate. Consequently, additional costs incurred in reducing congestion by increasing capacity must be compared with benefits resulting from shorter average waiting times to determine which of the available systems is most effective within budget constraints.

COMPUTING RESOURCES

A distinctive feature of computing resources, compared to many other economic goods, is that they are perishable. If a computer is "up" (i.e., in its operating state and thus ready to accept jobs) but idle, then the computing capacity that goes unused represents lost resources.[17] Although an organization may maintain a particular level of idle time intentionally, in order to obtain a higher quality of service for those jobs that are processed, an excess of unintentional idle time can result in costly waste, since unused computing capacity cannot be stored for future use. This underscores the importance of scheduling usage and why poor use of a computer's resources results in the need for greater capacity for any given level of input.

PREVIOUS WORK IN COMPUTER RESOURCE ALLOCATION

The advent of electronic computers created such problems as how computer resources should be made available to users. Solutions that have been proposed are characteristic of the disciplines from which they originate: Economists typically are interested in the use of pricing or pseudopricing mechanisms, operating in some market environment, to bring about the best distribution of resources among possible uses. The operations research analysts are less interested in inducing users to respond to market forces and more concerned with the characteristics of queueing systems that occur at a computer installation and with the development of efficient rules for assigning computer time to specific jobs of known characteristics.

[17]The effective capacity is the maximum utilization that will yield an acceptable service level to the user population. In a well-balanced batch system, the effective CPU capacity might be 70–80 percent of total available CPU cycles.

A number of articles and books that have appeared within the past 10 years address the many facets of allocating computer resources: fiscal control (planning and budgeting), market mechanisms (pricing and pseudopricing, such as priorities), sequential allocation (scheduling), two-level sequencing (macro- and microsequencing, as defined in Chapters 6 and 7, respectively), and value considerations.

Table 1 categorizes a number of recent publications relating to these five aspects of computer resource allocation. The authors usually address one or two categories, such as pricing and/or scheduling; occasionally, three or four categories are covered, but, prior to this work, no author incorporates all five aspects.[18] This situation is somewhat surprising since, as will be shown subsequently, each factor has major impact on resource allocation, whether it is explicitly considered or not. For example, any pricing scheme will be affected primarily by the funds available to users because, even if the scheduling rules provide acceptable service levels, demand is subject to the money on hand. Also, all scheduling rules imply an underlying statement about the relative value of jobs and user waiting time, as highlighted in Chapter 7. Similarly, different scheduling rules produce differing levels of service to specific users and, for a system where the user has some flexibility, affect when (or if) users demand service.

Perhaps the failure of researchers to develop a fully integrated approach has been due to the lack of a common thread linking all aspects of computer allocation. This is provided by the value function (see Chapter 6), a concept that enables derivation of the effects of pricing policies, priorities, budgets, scheduling rules, quotas, tariffs, computer speed, operating mode (such as batch and time-sharing), user environment, human behavior, and time itself on the overall effectiveness of computing for users in an organization. The approach allows computing needs and resources to be evaluated dynamically and adaptively and provides complete information to support decisions, unlike the partial answers of most previous methods.

PRESENTATION

Structure is crucial to this approach, as is demonstrated in Part I. In Chapter 2, a general organizational model is presented,

---

[18]In addition to the integration of the five aspects of computer resource allocation (shown in Table 1) into a single model, several other novel concepts are introduced in later chapters. These include the specification of a feedback loop between scheduling rules and

showing the relationships among users, management, and computer resources, the last of which are available from within the organization or from external suppliers. The relationships are described in terms of information transfer, money exchange, and the flow of computing services and physical hardware. Most computer environments are similar to the model described in Chapter 2, even if all components do not appear explicitly; for example, an organization may not have its own computer resources or, conversely, may not allow users to purchase external services, even though the potential for both options may exist.

A second structure is specified in the information, decision, and control model of Chapter 3, which traces fund allocation decisions for computing from the organizational level, to the computing function, to individual users. Within the computing function, type and quantity factors are presented. With respect to users, organizationally determined constraints, which serve to restrict and allocate computer usage, and the way in which users interact with computing availability are discussed. The dynamic nature of such a system is highlighted in an examination of factors affecting stability of user-computer interactions.

With organizational and allocative structures defined, the cost and value implications of such structures are examined in Part II. Beginning with Chapter 4, which discusses the meaning and measurement of costs and values relating to computing, procedures are developed for allocating computing resources from the long-term planning of computing availability from internal and/or external facilities (Chapter 5), through the medium-term control of demand for computing (Chapter 6), to the short-term operational scheduling of computer workloads (Chapter 7). The allocation procedures of Part II are based on the unique value function described in Chapter 4, which enables planning and control decisions of various time frames to be linked and to be treated dynamically.

In Chapter 8 of Part III, the propositions of Chapters 5, 6, and 7 are demonstrated with a series of computer models that illustrate the use of the value function concept in hypothetical, but realistic, environments. Examples of the application of the automated evaluation system relate to making organizational decisions about the use of computers of different capacities, the use of internal and/or external computers, and

---

user demand (Chapter 3); the application of the dynamic cobweb diagram to computer demand/service equilibrium (Chapter 3); the use of the value hill in scheduling, pricing, priority setting, service choice, and system selection decisions (Chapters 5, 6, and 8); and the value implications of scheduling rules (Chapter 7).

Table 1   Classification of Works on Computer Resources Allocation

Reference	Major Areas of Study				
	Fiscal Control (Budgeting)	Market Mechanisms (Pricing)	Sequential Allocation (Scheduling)	Two-Level Sequencing (Macro/Micro)	Value Considerations
Barr[a]		x			x
Coffman[b]			x		
Coffman and Kleinrock[c]			x		
Diamond and Selwyn[d]		x			
Dolan[e]		x	x		x
Ghanem[f]		x			x
Greenberger[g]			x		x
Kleinrock[h]			x		
Kriebel and Mikhail[i]	x	x			
Marchand[j]		x	x		x
Nielsen[k]		x	x		x
Sahney and May[l]			x	x	

Sharpe[m]	x	x
Singer, Kanter, and Moore[n]	x	
Smidt[o]	x	x
Smidt[p]	x	x
Streeter[q]	x	x
Vickrey[r]	x	x

[a] W. J. Barr. *Cost Effective Analysis of Network Computers.* Springfield, Va., National Technical Information Service, 1972.

[b] E. G. Coffman, Jr., ed. *Computer and Job-Shop Scheduling Theory.* New York, John Wiley and Sons, 1976.

[c] E. G. Coffman, Jr. and L. Kleinrock. "Computer Scheduling Methods and Their Countermeasures." In: *Proceedings of 1968 AFIPS Spring Joint Computer Conference, Atlantic City.* Montvale, N.J., AFIPS Press, 1968, pp. 11–21.

[d] D. S. Diamond and L. L. Selwyn. "Considerations for Computer Utility Pricing Policies." In: *Proceedings of 23rd National Conference, Association for Computing Machinery.* Princeton, N.J., Brandon/Systems Press, 1968, pp. 189–200.

[e] R. J. Dolan. "Priority Pricing Models for Congested Systems." Working Paper Series No. 7710. Rochester, N.Y., Graduate School of Management, University of Rochester, 1977. Mimeographed.

[f] S. B. Ghanem. "Computing Center Optimization by a Pricing-Priority Policy." *IBM Systems Journal, 14:*272–291, 1975.

[g] M. Greenberger. "The Priority Problem and Computer Time Sharing." *Management Science, 12:*888–906, July 1966.

[h] L. Kleinrock. *Queueing Systems, Volume 2: Computer Applications.* New York, John Wiley and Sons, 1976.

[i] C. H. Kriebel and O. I. Mikhail. "Dynamic Pricing of Resources in Computer Networks." In: *Logistics.* Edited by M. A. Geisler. Amsterdam, Elsevier/North-Holland, 1975, pp. 105–124.

[j] M. Marchand. "Priority Pricing with Application to Time-Shared Computers." In: *Proceedings of 1968 AFIPS Fall Joint Computer Conference, San Francisco.* Montvale, N.J., AFIPS Press, 1968, pp. 511–519.

[k] N. Nielsen. "Flexible Pricing: An Approach to the Allocation of Computer Resources." In: *Proceedings of 1968 AFIPS Fall Joint Computer Conference,* pp. 521–531.

[l] V. K. Sahney and J. L. May. *Scheduling Computer Operations.* Computer and Information Systems Monograph Series No. 6. Norcross, Ga. American Institute of Industrial Engineers, 1972.

[m] W. F. Sharpe. *The Economics of Computers.* New York, Columbia University Press, 1969, Chapter 11.

[n] N. Singer, H. Kanter, and A. Moore. "Prices and the Allocation of Computer Time." In: *Proceedings of 1968 AFIPS Fall Joint Computer Conference,* pp. 493–498.

[o] S. Smidt. "The Use of Hard and Soft Money Budgets, and Prices to Limit Demand for Centralized Computer Facility." In: *Proceedings of 1968 AFIPS Fall Joint Computer Conference,* pp. 499–509.

[p] S. Smidt. "Flexible Pricing for Computer Services." *Management Science, 14:*B581–B600, June 1968.

[q] D. N. Streeter. "Cost-Benefit Evaluation of Scientific Computing Services." *IBM Systems Journal, 11:*219–233, 1972.

[r] W. S. Vickrey. "Economizing and Pricing of Computer Services." Stanford, Calif., Center for Advanced Study in the Behavioral Sciences, 1968. Mimeographed.

the various rules for scheduling jobs through internal computers. Computer selection is of great concern to DP managers in their planning role, when they must balance the throughput capacity of computers of different speed against the cost. Sometimes the internal/external computing question is a matter of policy (i.e., "We will not use outside services if internal capacity is available!"). This decision, however, is closely tied to the computer selection process, since off-loading demand to outside computers can reduce the demand on internal computers. The value function approach illustrated in Chapter 8 provides a basis for developing the most effective policies with regard to external computer services and the size of internal computers. From an operational viewpoint, DP managers can see the effects of different scheduling rules on the value of work done, as determined through the examples. The automated evaluation system is a tool for experimenting with a host of scheduling rules and policies.

In Chapter 9, the implications of the concepts and examples presented earlier in the book are examined. These implications affect DP managers in their planning and control functions. Suggestions as to how management might implement some of the ideas are given, and possible extensions of the approach to other developing areas of DP management, such as distributed processing, data communications, word processing, and electronic mail, are proposed. For the operations researcher and computer scientist, Chapter 9 recommends methods for deriving new scheduling rules and examining the ways in which job value might vary. The use of scheduling characteristics as a basis for tuning computer systems also is described, as are a number of suggestions for further research into the behavioral aspects of scheduling. Finally, the extension of the approach to other fields of interest is proposed, and a selection of such fields is listed.

Some of the complexities pertaining to the definition of computer capacity are examined in Appendix A. Appendixes B and C present detailed heuristic procedures for applying some of the concepts described in Part II—the internal/external computer decision and control of the level and pattern of demand, respectively.

2

THE ORGANIZATIONAL STRUCTURE

An organization may be a commercial enterprise or an academic or public institution. It may be for profit or nonprofit. Its sole requirement here is involvement in at least one activity that presents a real or potential demand for feasible use of an electronic computer.

The information flows and control mechanisms that govern the allocation of computing resources depend on the structure of the organization. Although the basic concepts that will be introduced do not vary from one organization to another, their physical realizations do.

Harvath and Chilcoat describe how, over the past two decades, the typical systems (or computer) organization has changed from a somewhat isolated department reporting at a relatively low level in the organizational hierarchy to a broader function involved with more areas within the organization and reporting to high-level management.[1] Such differences still exist among various organizations today, in that the sophistication of DP management varies markedly from one organization to the next. At the same time, new forms of DP administration are taking shape. Consequently, a specific structure will be defined, and basic concepts will be developed within the framework of that structure; however, the ideas are general enough to be applicable in many other environments.

[1]C. Harvath and B. Chilcoat. *Bridging the Systems Expectations Gap.* New York, Amacom, 1973.

13

Whatever the organizational structure and relationships among those making computer-related decisions, the fundamental decisions are much the same. By addressing those decisions directly, the concepts become universal. The specification of a particular organizational structure merely facilitates the development of the ideas by placing them in context, but that in no way limits their application to other situations.

ORGANIZATIONAL STRUCTURE DEFINED

The structure of an organization represents the manner in which various functions have been compartmentalized into separate departments and divisions and the way in which the components are linked together.

Organizations have widely varied internal structures, and whether certain functions are centralized or decentralized depends on the specific function and the type of organization. Shubik defines the economic basis for decentralization as follows:

The concept of decentralization deals with the possibility of delegating decision making to more than one location in an organization. An optimally decentralized system will have the property that the net effect of all individual actions will be more favorable to the firm than the actions selected by any other array of decision centers. This must take into account costs of messages and organization and the possibilities of committing errors when decisions which appear to be locally optimal are not of benefit to the organization as a whole.[2]

Scott Morton[3] distinguishes between physical and logical (similar to organizational and functional) centralization and decentralization in his discussion of the "information function," and defines the following four combinations:

1. *Logical and Physical Centralization:* large central computer, central systems staff, and central priority setting
2. *Logical Centralization, Physical Decentralization:* central pro-

---

[2]M. Shubik. "Incentives, Decentralized Control, the Assignment of Joint Costs and Internal Pricing." In: *Management Controls: New Directions in Basic Research.* Edited by C. P. Bonini, R. K. Jaedicke, and H. M. Wagner. New York, McGraw-Hill, 1964, p. 210.

[3]M. S. Scott Morton. "Organizing the Information Function for Effectiveness as well as Efficiency." Paper presented to the Society for Management Information Systems Conference, New York City, September 1975.

gramming and decisions on what to do; local computers, perhaps minicomputers

3. *Logical Decentralization, Physical Centralization:* remote access to large central machine; user has decisions on what and how to build

4. *Logical and Physical Decentralization:* local computers; local control over what to do

Until recently, organizations that had their own internal computer facilities usually centralized computer resources, due to the high cost of hardware, the significant economies of scale, and a choice of equipment that was limited to medium and large machines. With the recent advent of minicomputers, intelligent terminals, distributed processing, and advanced networking systems, coupled with a continuing rapid decline in computer processing costs (on a cost per computation, per unit of memory, and of other bases),[4] the local processor is becoming more feasible technologically and competes favorably with larger units with respect to cost.

The topics of functional and organizational centralization and decentralization currently are receiving a great deal of attention in the computer press and at conferences.[5] Although the technical capability undoubtedly is available, the problem of distributed management and dispersed expertise remains, since economies of scale strongly affect the organization of personnel for data processing. Furthermore, the need for coordination among remote processors and consistency in selection, feasibility, and profitability decisions suggests that some determinations should still be made centrally, even for the physically decentralized approach.

Consequently, the functionally (or logically) centralized mode will be adopted for the models developed in the following paragraphs, as will the physically centralized computer center, although the latter specification may be relaxed without loss of generality. The general structure of the organization, however, is a divisionalized type, with individual users acting autonomously, subject to the control measures administered by a central controlling authority.

The Computer Center

In a decentralized organization, computing facilities may comprise a separate division servicing other divisions, or each division

---

[4]See M. Phister, Jr., *Data Processing Technology and Economics,* Santa Monica, Calif., Santa Monica Publishing Company, 1976, for trends in computer costs.

[5]For example, see C. E. Gabriel, "Some Common Problems Facing Management," *Infosystems,* 25:92–129, February 1978.

may support its own computer center. A computer center is defined here as a centralized computing facility under the control of a central authority. The functional area of computing may consist of an internal computer center or access to external computing facilities or a combination of both. The services available from the computer center are referred to as *internal computer services,* and those available from computer installations outside the control of the organization are called *external computer services.*

It is assumed that the computer center supplies services only to users within the organization; that is, the services of the computer center are an *intermediate good.* Although computing is embodied in the final product of the organization, it is not sold as a final product. Computer services purchased by the organization from an external source are considered to be a final product of the service supplying them. The final-product situation is not analyzed explicitly, although inferences as to the effect of the models in such cases can be made easily. The main difference is that the supplier of external computer services does not control the budgets of users and probably is unable to obtain information regarding the users' value functions (see Chapter 6).

The area of computing in an organization may not include an internal computer; that is, it may consist only of externally supplied computing services. Nevertheless, the decisions relating to the use of such services still are regarded as part of the computer function.[6]

The Central Control Division

The functions of the central control division include the administration of the computing budget and control over the allocation among users of computing resources purchased within this budget (see Chapter 3).

The physical realization of central control may be a department within the administrative division of a decentralized organization, if the computing function is considered to be centralized, or a department within a functional division, if the computing function is restricted to control within the division. Furthermore, the responsibilities of central control may be dispersed among several areas of the organization.[7] For

---

[6]A new type of manager, the time-sharing administrator, is appearing in organizations, with the role of controlling the use of external computer services. See, for example, D. E. Hummer, "The Role of the Time-Sharing Administrator," *Interactive Computing, 3*:3, November–December 1977.

[7]Observers have noted the recent appearance of organizational departments that perform

example, a controller with the responsibility of dividing the computing budget between internal and external services may be located at the administrative headquarters, whereas the computer operations personnel responsible for providing computer services to users may be located at the computer center.

For the purposes of this book, it is assumed that central control is characterized by its functions rather than its actual structural form.

The User Population

The user population includes those individuals within the organization who have an existing or potential need for computing and are authorized to make use of available computer services. The latter condition ensures, to some degree, that users' perceived needs coincide with organization goals.

A user is a component of the user population. A user may be more than one person or one person may be perceived to be several users; however, a one-to-one relationship usually will be adequate for this discussion. For example, normally, a computer center that uses a system based on account numbers will assign an account number to each individual; in some cases, an individual may have several account numbers, each for a different aspect of his work. In contrast, an account holder may authorize use of his account number to several other individuals when they are working together on a project.

Jobs

A job is a quantum of computer usage. It is a unit of demand that contains all the necessary components for servicing by a computer facility.

In the batch-processing mode, a job is not subject to user intervention while it is being processed. In a real-time interactive system, a job is interpreted to be a single "session" during which the user is on-line. In circumstances where the job undergoes identical processing in either mode, a user may accomplish several runs of a program (that would be considered as several jobs for batch processing) in a single interactive session. To simplify this presentation, only the batch-processing mode

---

many central control functions. T. Scannell, in "Information Resource Manager Seen Coming," *Computerworld, 11*(49):15, December 5, 1977, reports on the prediction that many organizations will employ an "information resource manager" to integrate decision making in the systems area. An extension of this forecast is the "computer resource manager," who would integrate all decisions relating to computing.

will be analyzed; however, real-time sessions can be considered as surrogate batch jobs with their own processing characteristics, and batch jobs activated through the real-time mode can be interpreted as separate jobs.

JOB CATEGORIES

Typically, there are three categories of jobs that are processed for an organization's users: scheduled production jobs, nonscheduled production jobs, and nonscheduled nonproduction jobs. Scheduled means that the start (and possibly, completion) times of particular jobs are specified before they are submitted for processing. This does *not* mean that nonscheduled jobs are not schedulable— merely that, in a typical data-processing environment, they are submitted without having a predetermined start time. A completion time, however, might be specified (see Chapter 7).

The difference between production and nonproduction jobs is that the former type of job must be run at some time, whether that time is specified or not, whereas the latter might be omitted from processing if circumstances indicate that it is beneficial to do so. Proposed production jobs fall into the nonproduction category in the planning stage since, prior to implementation, they can be cancelled. Also, obsolete production jobs may be classified as nonproduction and removed from the workload.

A fourth possible category might be scheduled nonproduction jobs. In practice, nonproduction jobs usually are not scheduled, because the number of runs and their outcomes are usually unpredictable. Rather, in a production environment, a quantity of computer resource is generally "blocked out" over a predetermined period expressly for development (or test) users.

In research and/or time-sharing environments with few scheduled jobs, users ordinarily will try to obtain access to computer resources at their convenience.

The concepts presented in this book originally were developed for a research environment with little production work, where most users exercise considerable discretion with respect to what jobs they run and when they run them. At first, it appeared that, since a scheduled production-oriented environment allowed little user flexibility, the models would not be as useful; however, the idea that a production environment is completely inflexible is a fallacy that is perpetuated by demanding users. Although some work must be constrained within narrow time limits, even critical production work can be adjusted if an effort is made. In later chapters, approaches will be described for evaluating how much effort is worthwhile. Second, in the system- and application-planning stages, there is a much greater degree of flexibility than when the production jobs and supporting procedures have been implemented.

In summary, these models and techniques, which will be further developed, are extremely useful in a wide range of processing environments and have the greatest influence in situations where planners, administrators, or users have flexibility with respect to what jobs are run and when they can be run.

THE SIZE OF A JOB

A job consists of a series of computer operations. The correspondence between an instruction to the computer contained in a computer program and the number of computer operations equivalent to that instruction varies with both the computer hardware and software, as does the speed with which the computer operations are performed. As Nielsen points out, "in today's multiprogrammed and/or time-shared computing environments there is no single resource that can be priced in order to allocate the usage of the entire system, for there are a multitude of resources which must be allocated."[8] Thus the size of a job may be defined in significantly more complex terms than merely the time it has occupied the computer. In more complicated situations, the size of the job may be defined as the amount of resources that the job actually uses or "otherwise renders unavailable to others."[9] A practical method of measuring job size is to use standard jobs to indicate the relative speed of different computer systems,[10] and then to interpolate to determine the relative size of the job.

THE JOB TYPE

A job may be characterized by such features as:

1. The programming language in which it is written
2. The physical nature of the input and output (e.g., cards, paper tape, or magnetic tape)

---

[8]N. Nielsen. "Flexible Pricing: An Approach to the Allocation of Computer Resources." In: *Proceedings of 1968 AFIPS Fall Joint Computer Conference, San Francisco.* Montvale, N. J., AFIPS Press, 1968, pp. 521–531.
[9]*Ibid.*, p. 522.
[10]See W. F. Sharpe, *The Economics of Computers,* New York, Columbia University Press, 1969, pp. 314–322, for a discussion of economies of scale in computing and the relative costs of computer systems.

3. The relative emphasis on certain processes (e.g., input-output bound or compute bound jobs in multiprogramming systems)

4. The type or status of the user submitting the job

The effect of job types on sequencing rules is important. For example, for a single-programming system, if jobs incur different setup times and costs depending on the type of the preceding job, the sequencing rule may depend heavily on the different job types. Similarly, for a multiprogramming system, scheduling may be affected significantly by the selection of job combinations, based on the comparative use of different parts of the system by jobs of different types.

THE VALUE OF JOBS

The question of value determination will be considered at length in Chapter 4. The value of a job need not be related directly to either its size or type: rather, a job's value may be a function of its time of submission, turnaround (or response) time, quality of service, diversity of service options, and so forth.

The Capacity of the Computer Facility

The *capacity* of a computer depends on its size, configuration, operational efficiency, specific mode of operation (e.g., single- or multiprogramming, interactive or batch processing), and sizes and types of jobs being processed. The capacity available for discretionary use (e.g., research or development) is dependent on the number, size, and type of nondiscretionary production jobs. Also, there are technological factors that permit only certain configurations of the units of the system and that restrict certain modes of operation to installations of specific configuration and size.

A possible definition of capacity is throughput, which is a measure of the number of standard jobs that may be processed per unit time. The number of operations that the central processing unit can perform per unit time may be obtained from the manufacturer's specifications, but usually this may not be translated directly into the throughput of the system because the typical system comprises a complex combination of modular units. In Appendix A, a comparison of two different configurations that have the same throughput indicates that the characteristics of each configuration can differ significantly under certain load conditions.

USER BUDGETS

In managerial accounting, budgeting is considered "the tool by means of which management plans are translated into financial terms and evaluated in relation to financial criteria."[11] Although this definition may be applied to the total computing budget, the major references to the term "budget" will be in the context of "user budget," which represents an upper limit on the quantity of resources that may be purchased by the user.

A user budget is a medium of exchange that is allocated to a user by central control. It is considered both a constraining and a control device that constrains by setting an upper limit to expenditures and controls by specifying the uses to which it can be applied.

In the following paragraphs, two specific restrictive distinctions, hard and soft budgets, are defined. Other budget features will be examined in Chapter 3.

Hard and Soft Money Budgets

Hard and soft money budgets are defined within an organizational context; that is, hard money may be spent either within or outside the organization, and soft money may be used only within the organization.[12] Consequently, soft money budgets usually are strictly internal currency, and the specification of a budget as soft money imposes a restriction of the funds to internal use.

Restricted and Unrestricted Budgets

The distinction between restricted funds and unrestricted funds is that the former are limited to specific predetermined uses,

---

[11]W. D. Knight and E. H. Weinwurm. *Managerial Budgeting*. New York, Macmillan, 1964, p. 5.

[12]See S. Smidt, "The Use of Hard and Soft Money Budgets, and Prices to Limit Demand for Centralized Computer Facility," in: *Proceedings of 1968 AFIPS Fall Joint Computer Conference*, p. 501. Smidt's usage of these terms derives from international monetary parlance: a hard currency is universally acceptable and easily convertible, whereas a soft currency is not easily convertible and is restricted in its use to a limited geographic area. Thus, Smidt considers hard money as that which "can be spent for any purpose" and soft money as funds that may be used "only in some limited way." He does not distinguish between the spatial acceptability of money (i.e., the restrictions on the places in which it may be spent) and its usage restriction (i.e., the limitation on the purposes to which it may be put). In this book, the hard/soft distinction refers to location; the restricted/unrestricted difference, to the particular use.

whereas the latter may be applied to any organizationally acceptable uses determined by the recipient of the budget. Both hard and soft money budgets may be either restricted or unrestricted. The distinction between the destination of funds (internal or external to the organization) and the purposes to which they may be applied is made to clarify the categorization of budgets. The resulting combinations of budget constraints are shown in Table 2.

Computer Funds in Practice

Whether an organization is for profit or nonprofit or an academic/research institution, government agency, manufacturing firm, or service organization usually makes a significant difference in the means by which computer activities are funded.

For example, the question of inside or outside monies arises in a university setting where general revenues are obtained from donations, government grants, and student tuition fees, and where specific research grants might come from foundations, government, and other sources. Typically, the funds to set up the computer center come from general revenues, and student and faculty users are assigned specific budgeted amounts of soft money. Outside money can be used to purchase computer services from the computer center or from outside sources. Sometimes the supplier of outside funds (especially the Federal Government) demands that it be charged for internal computer

Table 2   Categories of User Budgets

Description	Scope of Expenditure
Unrestricted Hard	Within and/or outside the organization, for *any* purpose expected to contribute to the net utility of the organization
Restricted Hard	Within and/or outside the organization, for *specified* purpose(s)
Unrestricted Soft	Within the organization *only*, for *any* purpose expected to contribute to the net utility of the organization
Restricted Soft	Within the organization *only*, for *specified* purpose(s)

services according to specific rules, as described in the section on average-cost pricing in Chapter 3.

Many administrators of academic institutions and, to a lesser extent, business organizations are reluctant to use general revenues for external computing if internal capacity is available, particularly in tight fiscal circumstances. The efficacy of such a decision is discussed in Chapter 5.

Inside and outside monies in academic institutions are analogous to nonbillable and billable charges in business. Computer use attributable to the operation and maintenance of the computer itself usually is not charged to users directly but is built into the billing rates. The outside monies in this case are the budgeted funds assigned to user divisions or departments, which are billed at standard rates for use of the computer. Nonbillable use includes computer activities relating to the administration of the business, such as payroll.

This billable/nonbillable distinction does not necessarily tie in with the hard money/soft money categories. For instance, use of the internal computer, which frequently is bought with soft money, may be nonbillable if the use is an overhead application and billable if the use can be charged to a profit center. If the internal computer facility is considered to be a profit center, with users free to spend computer funds internally or externally, then charges, in the form of transfer prices, are made in hard money—which is how the computer center obtains funds for its own operation. For the computer center itself, equipment, software, and other needs are bought with hard money.

The computer center staff's use of the computer for maintenance and support purposes is purchased with soft money, when such use is recorded in the accounting system. If the overhead functions of the business (finance, planning, personnel, and administration) use external computer services, they pay for them with hard money even though the functions are nonbillable and are part of the administrative expense of running the business. When a profit center, particularly one that charges its customers on a cost-of-service basis, uses external services, such computer services are directly billable, as they would be for internal computer use.

THE SPECIFIC STRUCTURE OF THE ORGANIZATION

The organization is assumed to consist of a number of divisions, of which the computer center is one. The internal computer facility supplies services to internal users only, making computing an intermediate good embodied in the final products of the organization.[13] Internal users may be affiliated with any part of the organization.

The Functions Of The Divisions

CENTRAL CONTROL

The central control division governs the entire computing function of the organization through the use of control measures that it enforces on the computer center and the internal user population. The objective of the central control division is to optimize the sum of the net values of all jobs run in a given period by means of budgetary and pricing controls.

THE COMPUTER CENTER

The computer center takes a passive role in the selection of jobs for processing and the times at which they enter the system. It is, however, responsible for the assignment of its budget to provide internal computing services and for the sequencing of jobs that arrive for service at the internal computer facility, the objective of both tasks being to maximize the total net value of jobs processed in a given period.

THE INTERNAL USERS

Users respond to the budget and price rules and the quality of service presented to them so as to maximize the values of their own computing jobs.[14]

EXTERNAL COMPUTER SERVICES

Computer services that are outside the direct control of the organization supply the organization with a schedule of prices and quality of service characteristics and can provide the organization any reasonable level of demand at the stated price and service standard.

---

[13]In cases where computing is the final product of an organization, the business sets a price for computer services based on a standard economic analysis. For an intermediate good, a measure of the value of services is not obtainable from the revenues received, as would be the case when the computer services are sold as a final good.

[14]The quality of service may be expressed in a number of ways with regard to reliability, convenience, speed of service, and so forth. It is assumed that the major characteristics that determine the quality of service are features of the probability distribution of turnaround time, such as its expected value, variance, or an upper percentile bound.

Computer-Related Functions in Practice

In business, a division might be a subsidiary, an operating unit, or a business unit. For example, a bank might divide itself according to the type of function performed, such as domestic banking operations, investment trusts, and international activities. Each division may have its own computer operation, or a centralized computer facility may serve all divisions. The choice between centralized or decentralized computer facilities depends on the size of the operation, the locations of the users, and the management's philosophy on security and control.

Universities usually are divided into departments based on field of interest; government agencies, by function. Such institutions generally have a centralized computer facility, with the individual departments purchasing computer services from the computer center. In some instances, a department, such as the physics or astronomy department, might have its own computer center for specialized work requiring equipment of a type different from standard data-processing machines. This specialization also holds true in business, particularly for process-control computer applications, as in the steel and chemical industries, and for research and development applications, as in the oil and pharmaceutical industries.

In all of these cases, when a central computer center is established, the divisions can be considered as suppliers of users, from both a functional and accounting perspective. In a university, the computer center will either be a separate unit or, more often, be affiliated with the computer science department of the institution. In a corporation, the computer operations unit usually will report to an administrative or financial function. As the computer function is becoming more integrated into the primary activities of corporations, the position of the head of computer operations is rising in corporate hierarchies.[15]

Users not only come from the various divisions of the organization but also from the computer center staff. A computer center system support staff typically handles such aspects of computer operations management as the maintenance and control of procedures for accessing and using the computer resources by (1) assigning long-term resources (such as disk packs) to particular users or classes of users, (2) assigning access codes to users and user departments for control and charging purposes, (3) maintaining the operating software in good working order, and (4) resolving problems arising from operating procedures or software. Usually, the support staff also will be responsi-

[15]See C. Harvath and B. Chilcoat, *Bridging the Systems Expectations Gap.*

ble for the accounting procedures by which users are charged for services. Since these support activities can use a considerable amount of computer resources, the support staff must be considered a significant user group.

The Flows of Information, Goods, and Services

Components of the structural model are linked by the flows of information, goods, and services between them. The various divisions and the interdivisional flows are shown in Figure 1. The goods and services that flow between divisions are in the form of media of exchange and computing services, respectively.

The central control division allocates the total computing budget partly to the computer center for the acquisition of hardware and software and the running of the computer installation and partly to external computer services through the intermediary of the user population.[16] Soft money is a resource-allocating device and does not represent the actual expenditure of cash by the organization, whereas expenditures on the internal computing facility and on external services are cash outlays.

The central control division receives information about the quality of service of the internal and external computer facilities, as well as the price schedule for external services. It then transmits a schedule of charges for running jobs on the internal computer installation to the user population. The users obtain the pricing schedule and service standards from the external services, as well as the internal quality of service characteristics. They compare prices and service levels and then submit their jobs to the internal and external computer facilities, depending on their assessment of the relative value rendered by the respective services.

SUMMARY

In this chapter, the components that make up the organizational structure were determined and a model was developed of the allocation of computing resources within such a structure. The flows of information, goods, and services through the system were indicated, and the functions of the decision-making units were described. This system will be considered in greater detail in the next chapter.

[16]In this general description of the organizational structure, both internal and external computer services are included; however, the analysis of Chapter 5 indicates that one or the other source of supply may be excluded in the most effective system.

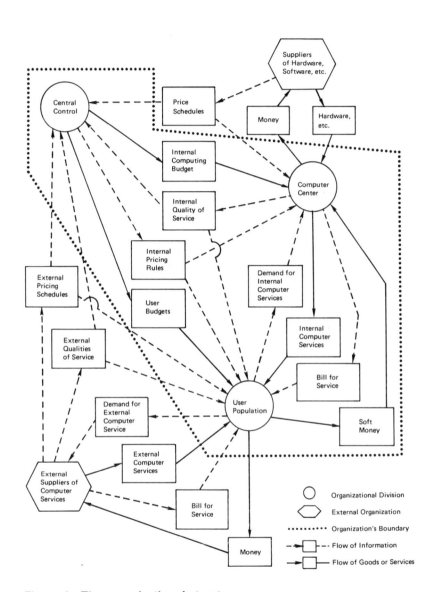

Figure 1   The organizational structure.

3
THE
CONTROL
MODEL

Having defined the organizational structure within which the allocation system operates, a model of the control system that governs the allocation of computing resources within such an organization will be developed in detail.

THE DECISION ASPECTS OF THE MODEL

Assignment of the Total Organizational Budget

Since computing represents only one of the activities of the organization, organizational headquarters must determine the total organizational budget and the percentages of the budget to be allocated to computing and noncomputing uses. The procedure that is adopted to assign funds to particular uses is termed *internal capital rationing*. Two types of capital rationing are defined by Bierman and Smidt:

1. A cutoff rate of return that is higher than the organization's cost of money is determined. Investments yielding returns greater than the cutoff are accepted, assuming that sufficient funds are available at the organization's cost of money, whereas investments with a return lower than the cutoff are rejected.
2. The total amount of funds committed to particular uses in a given period is limited to a specific quantity. The amount may be determined as a result of a present value or a rate of return analysis.[1]

[1]H. Bierman, Jr. and S. Smidt. *The Capital Budgeting Decision*. 4th Edition. New York, Macmillan, 1975, p. 152.

A basic premise is that organizational headquarters is aware of all profitable investment opportunities and that its objective is to maximize the profit from its activities by assigning funds effectively to both computing and noncomputing uses subject to budgetary constraints. This is shown as the "total budget allocation decision" in Figure 2. Knowing the value (or return on investment) of all potential investments, organizational headquarters determines how much should be spent on computer-related functions. In a decentralized organization, this decision could be made at the divisional level; headquarters would determine the division's total budget but would not stipulate its specific use. In this case, the process shown in Figure 2 might apply to each division. The computer central control function could still be centralized or not; however, if centralized, it would receive part of its total computing budget from each division requiring computer services. Table 3 reflects the budgetary decision processes shown graphically in Figure 2 and facilitates the direct comparison of the features of each decision.

Assignment of the Total Computing Budget

The computing budget is defined as that part of the organization's total budget that is devoted to computer-related activities in a given time period. The central control division allocates the total computing budget designated by organizational headquarters between internal and external computing services. This process is identified as the "internal facility versus external services budget allocation decision" in Figure 2. The decision as to how money is to be allocated for internal or external computing is based on the values of computer jobs available for processing and the characteristics (such as quality of service, cost of service, and so forth) of both the internal facility and the available external services. Maximization of the net value of computer jobs run in a given planning period is the objective,[2] as indicated in Table 3.

In Chapter 5, a specific example will be considered of the computer budget allocation decision when the characteristics of the available computing facilities are given.

[2]The term net value means the value of a job, less the money cost of processing it. The total net value in a given period is the sum of the values of all jobs run during the period minus the amount of the computing budget spent during the period, assuming that the latter includes all costs directly attributable to computing. The opportunity costs incurred are included in the value functions of the jobs in the form of value losses (see Chapter 4).

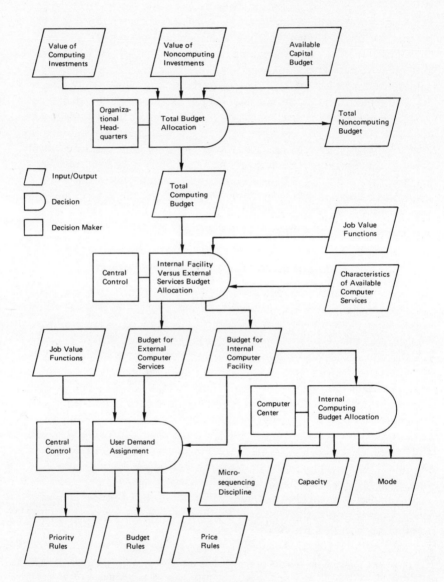

Figure 2   The budgetary decision process.

Table 3　Budgetary Decisions and Their Features

Name of Decision (Decision Maker)	Inputs	Constraints	Decision Variables	Objective	Description
Total budget allocation (organizational headquarters)	Value of potential computing and noncomputing investments	Capital rationing	Total computing budget; Total noncomputing budget	Maximize net value of all activities	Determination of the total budget available to the organization, and the allocation of the budget to maximize net value in a given period
Internal facility versus external services budget allocation (central control)	Job values with respect to computing service level; Internal and external computing characteristics	Total computing budget	Internal computing budget; External computing budget	Maximize net value of jobs run in a given period	Allocation of total computing budget between internal computer facilities and external computer services to maximize net value of jobs run in a given period
User demand assignment (central control)	Job value functions; Computing budget	Total computing budget not allocated to computer center; Internal computing capacity	User budget characteristics; User priority characteristics; Price structure	Maximize net value of jobs run in a given period	Allocation of general computing demand to maximize net value of jobs run in a given period
Internal computing budget allocation (computer center)	Job value functions; Equipment characteristics	Total computing budget	Capacity; Mode; Sequencing rules	Maximize net value of jobs run in a given period	Allocation of budget among hardware, software, and other resources to maximize net value of jobs run in a given period
Macrosequencing (user population)	Job values; Prices; Budgets; Priorities; Turnaround	User budgets; Budget restrictions	Level and pattern of demand for internal computing; Level and pattern of demand for external computing	Maximize net value of jobs run in a given period	Assignment of computing demand by users between internal and external facilities to maximize net value of jobs run in a given period

Assignment of User Demand

Although central control might determine the preferred allocation of computing between internal and external facilities in a given period, the user population (which is assumed to be somewhat autonomous) must be *induced* to use available computing facilities in a manner consistent with the organization's objective of maximizing the net value of all computer jobs run. This objective is achieved by central control through the use of budgetary control, pricing rules, and priority classifications. These three devices can be used to control both the average level of demand for computer services and the distribution of this demand over time for both internal and external computer services. The role of each of the three devices is considered in greater detail on pages 37 to 50, and specific rules and their effects are examined in Chapters 5, 6, and 7 and Appendixes b and c.

The "user demand assignment decision," shown in Figure 2 and Table 3, consists of the allocation of a user budget, the determination of pricing rules, and the assignment of user or job priorities. This function provides fine tuning of the coarser "internal facility versus external services budget allocation decision" and controls the level and timing of demand for, and selection of, computer services through persuasion rather than direct restrictions.

Internal Computing Budget Allocation

Typically, the computer center receives a budget for the provision of internal computer services, namely, capital equipment (buildings, computer hardware)—"capacity" in Figure 2; equipment support (software, operating personnel)—"mode" in Figure 2; and service support (equipment, software, and personnel controlling the quality of service)—"microsequencing discipline" in Figure 2.[3] The goal of the computer center manager is to select a combination of equipment, equipment support, and service support that will result in the greatest expected net value of computer jobs run in a given period.

---

[3]Microsequencing rules determine the sequence in which jobs that have arrived at the computer center for service are *run*. Macrosequencing is the process by which the sequence in which jobs *arrive* at the computer center is effected. Similar terminology is adopted in V. K. Sahney and J. L. May, *Scheduling Computer Operations*, Computer and Information Systems Monograph Series No. 6, Norcross, Ga., American Institute of Industrial Engineers, 1972, p. 5, where "microscheduling" has the same meaning as microsequencing but where "macroscheduling" means the scheduling of work to and beyond the computer room, which is a different concept from macrosequencing.

Macrosequencing

Each user, in selecting when and where to submit jobs and which jobs to have processed, is assumed to respond autonomously to the level of demand for internal computer services (and resultant turnaround time) as it varies over time; to the availability of both internal and external services; and to prices, budgeted funds, and organizational restrictions. Users are assumed to respond to exogenous factors to maximize the net value of computer jobs run in a given period, as described for the macrosequencing decision shown in Table 3 and in the computer usage allocation model illustrated in Figure 3. The macrosequencing decision is described in detail in Chapter 5, which also discusses the internal versus external decision, and in Chapter 6, which covers the demand level and demand distribution over time. An overview of the computer usage allocation model is presented in the following section.

COMPUTER USAGE ALLOCATION MODEL

This section considers the specific functional relationships that arise from the physical characteristics of the system. These relationships, shown in the computer usage allocation model (Figure 3), correspond specifically to the various time distributions of the system—processing, queueing, and turnaround times.

Processing Time

The time required to process a particular job on a computer will depend on some or all of the following:

1. Computer capacity (e.g., rate of throughput, processing speed)
2. Processing mode (e.g., single programming or multiprogramming, batch or interactive, real or virtual storage)
3. Microsequencing discipline (if setup times vary with job sequence or if jobs are in contention for the same resources)

It is assumed that the computer capacity and mode are fixed throughout the short-term planning period but the microsequencing may be varied to respond to variations in the arrival pattern of job types. The processing time relationship is shown in the upper half of Table 4.

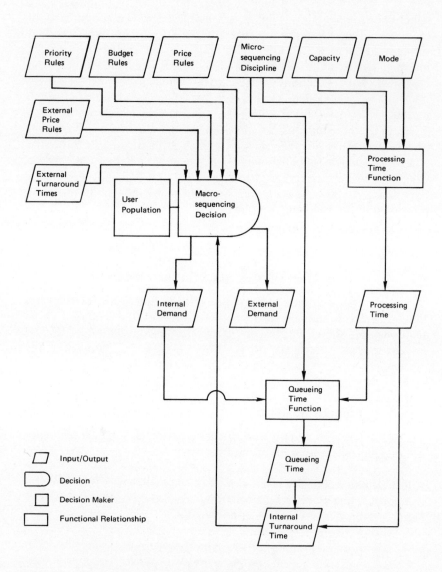

Figure 3   Computer usage allocation model.

Table 4 Processing and Queueing Time Relationships

Name of Function	Independent Variables	Dependent Variable	Description
Processing time	1. Microsequencing discipline 2. Capacity of computer facility 3. Processing mode	Processing time for job i, $i = 1, \ldots, n$	The time required to process a job depends on the rate of throughput (or capacity) of the computer facility, the processing mode (e.g., single- or multi-programming), and, if sequence affects the setup times of jobs, the micro-sequencing rules.
Queueing time	1. Level and distribution of demand 2. Microsequencing discipline 3. Processing times	Queueing time for job i, $i = 1, \ldots, n$	The time spent waiting in the queue by the job, that is, the time interval from the arrival of the job at the computer facility until it begins service. The queueing time depends on the arrival pattern of jobs, the processing times of arrivals, and the microsequencing rules.

Queueing Time

The queueing (or waiting) time for a particular job is the interval between the time the job arrives at the computer facility and the time it begins service. The queueing time depends on the properties of other jobs (such as arrival rate, pattern of arrivals, processing times) as well as the microsequencing rules in effect. The relationship between queueing time and other variables is shown in Table 4.

The queueing times of external services are independent of the demand of users in the organization if the organization's usage of any single external service represents a small fraction of the capacity of that service. If the organization's usage is a significant part of the external service's capacity, then the external queueing time will be a function of demand, as it will be for the internal queueing time. Such a relationship, the *congestion delay function,* is discussed later in this chapter.

Turnaround Time

The turnaround time of a particular job is defined as the sum of its queueing time and processing time, that is, the interval between the time the job is submitted to the computer center and the time at which it completes service.

The General System

The decision and allocative relationships combine to form the general system that is obtained by linking Figures 2 and 3. Figure 2 indicates the decision processes that determine the independent variables of the allocation functions of Figure 3. There are a number of implicit and explicit feedback loops in this overall process, as many of the inputs for the decision-making processes are generated from historic data that are fed forward from previous periods. For example, the budgetary and pricing rules specified by central control may be based, to some extent, on the performance of specific rules in prior periods or in other systems. The feedback of turnaround time into the user demand allocation decision may or may not occur within the given period. If not, an *open-loop* system results; otherwise, the *closed-loop* system, shown in Figure 3, is obtained. The desirability of explicitly introducing such a feedback loop into the control model is evaluated later in this chapter, when the stability of the system is considered.

Clearly, the implicit feedback of turnaround-time performance cannot be avoided in most cases, although tampering with the response time of systems has been suggested.[4]

THE BUDGET AS A CONTROL MEASURE

In accounting, a budget is defined as "a financial plan serving as a pattern for and a control over future operations";[5] that is, a budget may serve as a *plan* and as a *control*. Stedry states that the objective of budgetary control is to "increase long-run profit at the fastest possible rate."[6] The role of the user budget in the computer usage allocation model is to induce users to maximize the long-run net value of computing for the organization as a whole. This can be achieved through the manipulation of certain characteristics of the budget itself, such as its level, perishability, transferability, and destination.

The Budget Level

The user's budget determines the upper limit of the quantity of computing resources that can be purchased subject to a given price and priority structure. The total of all user budgets indicates the maximum possible level of demand for computing during the period. If the budget consists of hard money and external computing services are in unlimited supply, then the quantity of computing resources available to users is limited only by the size of the budget and the cost of services. If, however, users are given soft money budgets that can be used only for internal computer services, then central control can manipulate user demands by adjusting the total user budget

---

[4]One theory is to introduce a minimum response time into time-sharing systems so that, when response time increases beyond the minimum, users will not react as adversely as they might if the comparison was made between immediate response of an unloaded system and longer response time. See L. Wright, "A User Oriented Method of Computer Scheduling," presentation to the Northeast Region, Computer Measurement Group, New York, February 1978. Wright proposed a similar delaying tactic for batch systems in order to reduce the historical variation in turnaround time as the system load increases over time. Both approaches imply an aversion to the variance of turnaround time, which may be as great as or greater than the expected turnaround.

[5]E. Kohler. *A Dictionary for Accountants.* Englewood Cliffs, N.J., Prentice-Hall, 1956, p. 67.

[6]A. C. Stedry. *Budget Control and Cost Behavior.* Englewood Cliffs, N.J., Prentice-Hall, 1960, p. 2.

and/or the capacity of the facility. Central control can provide users with purchasing power to buy more (based on specific rate structures) than the available internal supply, but then the physical capacity of the installation becomes the constraining force.

In practice, users will attempt to obtain larger budget allocations than their anticipated needs to avoid the possibility of running out of money and the need to renegotiate another allocation of funds. On the other hand, central control tries to limit budget allocations to those uses that have the greatest return and to avoid giving users excess funds that may be expended on relatively low-return jobs. In such cases, if a bargaining mechanism exists within the organization, the final user budget allocation will depend on the relative bargaining powers of individual users and their negotiating strength versus that of other users competing for the same limited computing monies and central control.[7] Central control should relate its total user budget to the available internal capacity (particularly in the soft money case) and the percentage of allocated funds that it *expects* will be used.

Changes in the Budget Level

Since the quantity of computing resources that users can purchase depends on the magnitude of the total computing budget *and* the price schedule of services, the potential demand may be controlled either by budgetary or pricing means. When the price levels of external services are not within the control of the organization, central control is limited to budgetary control. A tariff, which might take the form of a surcharge levied by the organization on each dollar spent on external services, could be used if the organization wished to have partial control over external prices.

Potential user demand may be adjusted dynamically throughout the budget period to bring the actual level of demand closer to the desired level. If this objective is to be achieved, however, it is necessary to know how users will respond to the frequency of changes and the magnitude of changes relative to the base level.[8] Furthermore, the timing of particular changes can have a significant effect on the responses of the user population.[9]

[7]J. G. Cross. *The Economics of Bargaining.* New York, Basic Books, 1969. Cross develops an interesting analytical model of the bargaining process.

[8]A. C. Stedry, *Budget Control and Cost Behavior,* pp. 17–42, develops a mathematical model of a budget control system that relates changes in the budget to the behavior of the user.

[9]See J. C. Kinard, ''The Effect of Variations in the Timing and Ordering of Presentation

Budgetary means of dynamic control are more practical where there are relatively few individual user budgets. In this study, where there are conceptually many users, each with a budget applicable to computing, the many lines of communication necessary for implementing the budgetary method of control suggest that it generally would not be practicable; the use of pricing controls to regulate the level of demand over time would be more efficient.

The effectiveness of any budgetary rule is limited by the appropriateness of the pricing rule and vice versa. If a budget rule allocates funds beyond the profitable need of a user, the user is no longer constrained by pricing measures, since his utility of money is lower than that assumed by the pricing rule. It is important, therefore, to consider budgetary and pricing controls together and to integrate their mutual decisions.[10]

Perishability of the Budget

A user may be able to use his computing budget within the budget period in any convenient pattern; for example, he may use his budget evenly throughout the period or in a short interval, with negligible usage throughout the remainder of the period. If the budget period is long, relative to the average turnaround time of a job, central control may be unable to predict accurately the distribution of user demand over time, which could result in heavy value losses due to congestion at certain times in the internal facility (see Chapter 6). The value losses would be lower with a more even distribution of demand. One solution to this problem would be a reduction in the budget period to lessen the variance in demand level. Complex allocation of budgets can be expensive, however, so a trade-off must be made between the benefits of reduced variance and the additional costs of a more complicated budget allocation system.

Another approach is the use of a perishable budget, which decreases over time regardless of usage and is further reduced by the purchase of services. This avoids the buildup of large reserves of budgeted usage that, if demanded within a short interval, could overload the

of Otherwise Identical Information on Expectations," Doctoral Dissertation, Stanford, Calif., Graduate School of Business, Stanford University, 1969.

[10]This topic is dealt with from a practical standpoint in C. W. Axelrod, "The Computer Pricing Process," *CMG Transactions, 18*:3-2–3-13, December 1977. The pricing process is viewed as a complex series of decisions, beginning with a set of expenses and ending with a pricing policy, which have passed through a succession of allocation procedures.

internal system. Variation of the perishability parameters provides central control with another means of controlling demand.

The *transferability* of a budget is the transferring of budgeted funds among users, budget periods, or uses. The greater the flexibility of transferability, the less control the organization has over the level and pattern of nonscheduled user demand.

Destination Restrictions

In Chapter 2, the terms hard, soft, restricted, and unrestricted were defined as they pertain to budgeted funds. Hard money may be spent either within or outside the organization; soft money is limited to uses within the organization only. Restricted funds may be used only for specified purposes; unrestricted funds may be spent on any profitable use. The greater the restriction on the destinations of user budgets, the more accurate the forecasts of demand and the more effective the control can be; however, closer restrictions are more costly to impose and require more and better information to implement effectively.

The feasibility of such control techniques must be judged relative to their long-term contribution to profits (or cost reduction). Their validity depends on the quality of information available about system parameters and the predicted behavior of users.

CONTROL THROUGH PRICING

Surprisingly little has been written about the control of computing resources through budgetary means—greater emphasis has been placed on pricing techniques. Little regard has been given to the prerequisite distribution of income (i.e., budgets). Although the effects of most budgetary controls can be achieved through pricing, there are instances when budgetary controls are significantly superior (as in the case of restrictions of budgets to specific uses); therefore, a full treatment of price allocation also must include budgetary allocation and the budget/price interaction.

The Purpose of Pricing

Brown and Oxenfeldt have suggested that the function of prices differs depending on which point of view is being considered.[11]

[11]F. E. Brown and A. R. Oxenfeldt. "Should Prices Depend on Costs?" *MSU Business Topics,* 16:73–77, Autumn 1968.

Academic economists have considered prices as a device for allocating resources in some optimal fashion, rather than a cost recovery mechanism.[12] Businessmen select those prices that they expect will maximize the long-term profits of their firms, whereas government representatives stress the public welfare role of prices.[13] The primary purpose of pricing in this discussion is its role in allocating the demand for computing effectively.[14] The selection of a pricing mechanism depends on the budgetary controls in effect. Obviously, it is unnecessary to duplicate control measures.

The three major categories of pricing control used in the computer usage allocation model are:

1. The assignment of demand to internal and/or external suppliers of computing services (see Chapter 5 for an appropriate pricing rule)
2. The limitation of total demand level for computing in a given period
3. The regulation over time of the demand pattern for internal computer services (see Chapter 6)

Pricing control does not have to be used to channel demand to internal or external services in a soft money budget, since soft money is used only for internal services. Table 5, which indicates the functions of pricing rules for a variety of budgetary restrictions, shows that the more constraining the budgetary means of control, the more limited the role of pricing in resource allocation. Clearly, it is the combination of budget characteristics that determines the role of pricing policy.

PRICING RULES

A number of pricing rules for the allocation of internal computing resources that have been suggested and described extensively in the literature are discussed in this section. Some rules are based on the cost of running jobs, some on specific properties of the

---

[12]N. Singer, H. Kanter, and A. Moore. "Prices and the Allocation of Computer Time." In: *Proceedings of 1968 AFIPS Fall Joint Computer Conference, San Francisco.* Montvale, N.J., AFIPS Press, 1968, p. 494.

[13]J. R. Nelson. "Pricing and Resource Allocation: The Public Utility Sector." In: *Utility Regulation.* Edited by W. G. Shepherd and T. G. Gies. New York, Random House, 1966, pp. 58–87.

[14]Pricing also may be used to determine the sequence in which jobs are serviced once they have arrived at the computer facility. This is considered in the subsequent section, "Price-Priority Rules."

Table 5   Pricing Control for Various Types of User Budgets

Budget Type	Functions of Pricing Rule
Unrestricted Hard	1. Allocation of funds between computing and noncomputing uses 2. Allocation of computing demand between internal and external facilities 3. Limitation of maximum demand for computing 4. Regulation of demand pattern for internal computing
Unrestricted Soft	1. Allocation of funds between internal computing and noncomputing uses 2. Limitation of maximum demand for internal computing 3. Regulation of demand pattern for internal computing
Restricted* Hard	1. Allocation of computing demand between internal and external facilities 2. Limitation of maximum demand for internal computing 3. Regulation of demand pattern for internal computing
Restricted* Soft	1. Limitation of maximum demand for internal computing 2. Regulation of demand pattern for internal computing

*It is assumed that the use of funds is restricted to computing only.

system, and others on the values of jobs. The appropriateness of any rule depends on the characteristics of the particular system.

Cost-Based Pricing

The less complex cost-based rules consider only the costs directly attributable to the jobs themselves, whereas the more sophisticated rules also consider opportunity costs.

AVERAGE-COST PRICING

The popularity of average-cost pricing, especially in university computer centers, can be attributed in many cases to the insistence by government sponsors of computer-oriented work for its use. This pricing procedure requires that the total computing costs over a given period be assigned to individual jobs in direct proportion to the percentage of total usage that each represents. Since sponsored usage frequently represents a large percentage of total demand for the computer center's services, such sponsors often insist on this form of pricing to avoid subsidizing other computer users.

A major operational advantage of average-cost pricing is that the accounting calculations are relatively straightforward. It is necessary to maintain a record of costs and usage only, from which user charges can be obtained by simple ratio calculations. From the viewpoint of system effectiveness, however, this form of pricing has proved to have a number of serious faults.[15]

One disadvantage is that the actual prorated charges cannot be calculated until the pricing period is over. If predicted usage is the basis of *ex ante* pricing rates that are charged at the time of processing, then the revised *ex post* rates may differ considerably from the initial rates, requiring an account adjustment that might result in additional payments or refunds; either way, the uncertainty of the final cost throughout the period is undesirable. If users are billed at the end of the period, they will find it difficult to charge against their individual budgets during the period, since the actual charges will not be known. Another disadvantage is that the organization might be tempted to limit the use of the computer by internal users, thereby increasing the cost per unit of computing for both internal and external users.[16] This will increase the relative and absolute contribution of external users' funds to the computer center, assuming the level of external demand is not price sensitive.

As an example, if the cost of the computer center is $1 million per year, and it is anticipated that 100,000 units of use will be charged

---

[15]Several writers have considered the effects of average-cost pricing on the allocation of computer services. See, for example, H. Kanter, A. Moore, and N. Singer, "The Allocation of Computer Time by University Computer Centers," *Journal of Business,* *41*:375–384, July 1968; and B. E. Goetz, "The Effect of a Cost Plus Contract on Transfer Prices," *Accounting Review, 44*:398–400, April 1969.

[16]Note that this does not contradict the assumption that computing is an intermediate good since only internal users are permitted to use the internal computer facility. The sponsor acquires something that embodies computing rather than computer services themselves.

out—50,000 units to internal users and 50,000 units to external users— the cost per unit is $10. Here, the internal users will contribute $500,000, as will the external users. If the internal users are then limited to 30,000 units (by budgetary means, say), then total use is 80,000 units and the cost rises to $12.50 per unit. This results in a year-end adjustment in users' accounts to reflect the $2.50 increase in unit charges and an increase in external users' total contributions from $500,000 to $625,000.

Furthermore, the use of average-cost pricing encourages users to demand services from the internal computing facility during periods of heavy usage because of the resulting lower processing rates, which creates additional congestion. Average-cost pricing also discourages demand during periods of light workload since the low usage results in higher processing rates. These influences cause a divergence in the distribution of demand and supply for computer services, thereby reducing effectiveness.

A primary justification for using average-cost pricing would be the ease of calculating rates. Unless the computer center has no choice, however, due to sponsors' pressures, it is unlikely that this one advantage would outweigh the many disadvantages.

MARGINAL-COST PRICING

A microeconomic argument is that the profit-maximizing organization should produce up to, but not beyond, the level of output that yields the greatest profit in a given period. This is the level at which the marginal cost of production (the cost of producing one additional unit) is equal to the marginal revenue received (the revenue obtained from selling that additional unit), assuming that it is worthwhile for the organization to exist at all.[17] In a nonprofit situation, the analogous rule is that, in a given period, the marginal cost and the marginal value (i.e., the value of the additional unit redounding to the organization) should be equal, which leads to a maximization of the total net value of the organization.[18]

Marginal-cost pricing is not directly applicable to the control model, since the computing services generated by the model's internal facility represent an intermediate good and not a final product. A modified

---

[17]P. A. Samuelson. *Foundations of Economic Analysis.* Cambridge, Mass., Harvard University Press, 1955, p. 88.
[18]S. Smidt. "The Use of Hard and Soft Money Budgets, and Prices to Limit Demand for Centralized Computer Facility." In: *Proceedings of 1968 AFIPS Fall Joint Computer Conference,* p. 501.

marginal-cost analysis is appropriate in some cases, as is illustrated in the discussion on transfer pricing.

TRANSFER PRICING

The basic objective of transfer pricing is to determine the optimal price at which goods should be transferred between two autonomous profit centers of a decentralized organization, so that the operations of the organization are optimized globally.

Optimal internal pricing rules have been considered in a number of market situations by Hirshleifer, whose simplest example has two decentralized divisions: a manufacturing (or producing) division and a sales division.[19] The former is able to supply all of the intermediate good that the latter requires, with no external market to supply or demand the intermediate good. The marginal cost is assumed to be an increasing function of the output level for both divisions. All output units are identical, and the output is sold in a perfectly competitive market in which price is constant for all levels of output. Under these particular conditions, the optimal policy of the organization is to generate the level of final product at which the sum of the marginal cost of the manufacturing (or producing) division (curve MC_m in Figure 4) and of the sales division (MC_s) is equal to the constant price per unit of output (P), which is an output of OX units. In order to induce the producing division to sell OX units to the sales division, central control must set the transfer price at OA.

Several problems arise when this type of analysis is applied to computing services. The marginal cost of computer services typically is very small,[20] which leads to a paradox that is pointed out by Bierman:[21] If the marginal cost of the intermediate good, such as computing services, is constant with respect to output, then the producing division makes no profit if the transfer price is at its marginal cost. Furthermore, the transfer price does not provide the producing

---

[19]J. Hirshleifer. "On the Economics of Transfer Pricing," *Journal of Business*, 29:172–184, July 1956; "Economics of the Divisionalized Firm," *Journal of Business*, 30:96–108, April 1957; "Internal Pricing and Decentralized Decisions," in: *Management Controls: New Directions in Basic Research*, edited by C. P. Bonini, R. K. Jaedicke, and H. M. Wagner, New York, McGraw-Hill, 1964, pp. 27–37.

[20]This assumption occurs throughout computing literature. It is suggested that the high fixed costs of computing far exceed the variable costs, so the marginal operating costs are relatively negligible. See S. Smidt, "Flexible Pricing for Computer Services," *Management Science, 14*:B581–B588, June 1968.

[21]H. Bierman, Jr. *Topics in Cost Accounting and Decisions.* New York, McGraw-Hill, 1963, pp. 100–101.

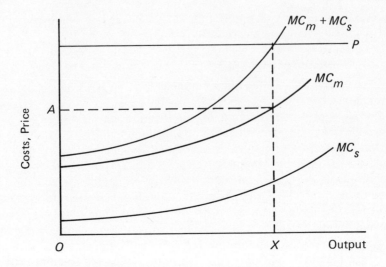

Figure 4   Determination of optimal output (OX) and transfer price (OA) for intermediate good, assuming perfect competition for the final product (price P) and no external market for intermediate good.

division with any guide as to optimal output because its profit is zero at all levels, as shown in Figure 5. The desired output is still OX units in this case, but this value results from the increasing nature of the MC_s curve.

Further problems arise when it is no longer assumed that the intermediate goods are homogeneous, identical, time-independent, and embodied in the final product in a fixed ratio and that final goods are homogeneous and independent of time. The resulting nonhomogeneous and time-dependent goods are typical of computer jobs. When the capacity is fixed, the optimal output of the intermediate good (with or without the existence of an intermediate market) can cause congestion in the system; therefore, the implications of opportunity costs arising from congestion delay must be considered. The almost constant marginal computing cost (equivalent to MC_m in Figure 5) would be appropriate only for low levels of output when there are negligible congestion costs. If delay costs are accounted for, the marginal computing cost curve would look more like MC_m in Figure 4. Although the marginal *operating* cost of computing may be constant and virtually zero, the marginal *opportunity* cost resulting from congestion in the system would be increasing with output for moderately to heavily loaded systems, so that the paradox of Figure 5 is avoided. Neverthe-

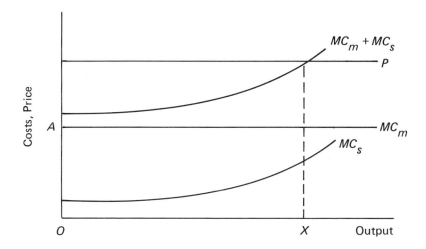

Figure 5 Optimal output cannot be determined at transfer price (OA) for intermediate good when marginal cost of manufacturing (or producing) division (MC_m) is constant with respect to output level.

less, even though the addition of opportunity costs to the marginal production cost allows the transfer price to determine the optimal output in this simplified case, the problems of nonhomogeneity and time sensitivity remain.[22]

Demand-Based Pricing

Some pricing systems relate to such factors as job characteristics, variation of demand over time, and specific needs of users.

[22]G. B. Dantzig and P. Wolfe, in "Decomposition Principles for Linear Programs," *Operations Research, 8*:101–111, February 1960, developed a computational method of decomposition that enables large linear programming problems to be broken down into segments. This technique has been adapted to decentralized decision-making situations to obtain internal transfer prices that lead to the optimization of a global objective function (W. J. Baumol and T. Fabian. "Decomposition, Pricing for Decentralization and External Economies." *Management Science, 11*:1–32, September 1964.) and to the quadratic programming problem (J. E. Hass. "Transfer Pricing in a Decentralized Firm." *Management Science, 14*:B310–B331, February 1968.) The decomposition approach is still limited to homogeneous, time-insensitive intermediate goods and, therefore, is not useful for evaluating computer services.

JOB CHARACTERISTICS AS A BASIS FOR PRICING

In a typical system, computer jobs impose a wide variety of demands on the facility: Some jobs require considerable intervention by the computer operator (such as tape mounting and loading of special forms into the printer), other jobs use only certain limited features of the system, and still others tie up specific pieces of equipment exclusively, thereby making parts of the system unavailable to other users.

Smidt, for example, considers the problem of determining prices for specialized services used only by certain users.[23] The pricing of various measures of system utilization, such as elapsed time, compute time, disk space, disk accesses, cards read, setups, and so forth, has been suggested by Nielsen,[24] and a number of commercial packages are available on the market to perform this type of pricing.

PEAK-LOAD PRICING

A peak-load pricing rule relates the price charged per unit of processing time to the expected level of demand at given intervals. This form of pricing originally was developed for the allocation of electricity to users by a utility,[25] but also has been applied to computer services.[26] The basic approach is to charge a relatively high rate during periods of high use to discourage users and reduce potential congestion in the system. Lower rates in off-peak periods aim to attract users and increase utilization. This equalizing of demand can reduce the capacity otherwise required to meet peak loads and can utilize more of the off-peak idle capacity, resulting in more efficient use of resources. If the peak-load pricing rule is responsive to users' true needs, and if users are able to alter their use of the system to increase the total net value of usage, effectiveness also will be increased. Tolls or vouchers may be used as surrogates for peak-load pricing. Tolls must be paid to gain access to the computer and can vary with user or job type, time of day, day of week, and so on. Vouchers are similar to tolls except that they are prepaid and, in a sense, act as a retainer that will ensure access when required. The computer center can predetermine the upper limit of access by using a voucher system. Both tolls and vouchers can be varied in magnitude over time.

[23]S. Smidt. "Flexible Pricing," pp. B595–B597.

[24]N. Nielsen. "Flexible Pricing: An Approach to the Allocation of Computer Resources." In: *Proceedings of 1968 AFIPS Fall Joint Computer Conference*, pp. 523–527.

[25]O. E. Williamson. "Peak-Load Pricing and Optimal Capacity Under Indivisibility Constraints." *American Economic Review*, 56:810–827, September 1966.

[26]S. Smidt. "Flexible Pricing," pp. B588–B593.

FLEXIBLE PRICING

The term flexible pricing generally is used for those pricing rules where rates vary in response to changes in one or more features of the system. This is different from rules that establish initial rates, ascribed to various features of the system, which do not respond to changes in the system. Thus, peak-load pricing may be flexible if it responds dynamically to changes in the level of demand, but it is not considered to be flexible if the rule adopts a predetermined rate schedule that remains unchanged for long periods.

The particular feature or features of the system that are linked to flexibility of price should relate to characteristics that are deemed important to the user or organization. For example, a user may be willing to pay any reasonable rate to assure service within a given time, or he may specify a maximum rate and accept whatever quality of service this might yield.[27]

Value-Based Pricing Rules

Some rules that have been proposed link price to the value of jobs, as in an auction system where users bid against one another to obtain the desired service.[28] Several value-based rules will be developed in subsequent chapters.

CONTROL THROUGH PRIORITY RULES

A further control mechanism is the multiple priority waiting line. A priority system requires that a higher priority job be given precedence over a lower priority job.

Budgetary Priority Rules

With budgetary priority rules, the priority category is an additional restriction on the budget. The different priorities may apply solely to microsequencing or may be used to control the time at which certain jobs may be run, which is analogous to the effect of peak-load pricing. This latter aspect of priorities will be considered further in Chapter 7.

---

[27]These are called the completion time specified (CTS) and maximum rate specified (MRS) rules by S. Smidt in "Flexible Pricing," pp. B586–B587.

[28]See, for example, N. Nielsen, "Flexible Pricing: An Approach," p. 527.

Price-Priority Rules

In the case of price-priority rules, different priorities are charged at different rates—the higher the priority, the higher the rate. In a purely price-based priority system, all users are able to purchase any level of priority that they desire and can afford. Control can be applied through budgetary manipulation, variation in the price-priority relationships, and price levels.

USER RESPONSE TO CONTROLS

With such complexity in control measures, it often is difficult to determine what combination of controls are most suitable in a particular situation. In Chapters 5 and 6, the effects of various controls on the user's decision as to when and where to submit his jobs will be examined. In Chapter 7, the effect of controls on the sequence in which jobs are submitted will be discussed.

THE STABILITY OF THE COMPUTER USAGE ALLOCATION MODEL

In a control system that incorporates a feedback loop, the question of stability should be considered. Feedback control has been defined to be present "whenever control is effected through the comparison of the *actual* output of a system with its *desired* output."[29] In the system shown in Figure 3, there is feedback of internal turnaround information into the macrosequencing decision.

In the computer usage allocation model, the internal level and pattern of demand—which are partially dependent on the internal turnaround—determine the internal turnaround times. For the system to be in equilibrium, the internal turnaround times, which are the input of the feedback loop to the users, must be equal to the internal turnaround times that result from the users' demands. The conditions that support a stable equilibrium and the parameters of the system that affect stability will be examined next.

[29]S. E. Elmaghraby. *The Design of Production Systems.* New York, Reinhold, 1966, p. 333.

Demand as a Function of Turnaround

It is postulated here that the level of demand at a given time depends on certain properties of the probability distribution of turnaround time: The greater the expected turnaround time and the larger the variance of the turnaround-time distribution at a given time, the smaller the level of demand. If the expected turnaround time for a job exceeds a certain limit, it would no longer be profitable for the user to submit the job, since the cost of waiting would exceed the value of running it. High uncertainty (or variance) in the time at which the job will complete processing is assumed to result in losses in user efficiency and convenience. One study found that user demand is a decreasing function of maximum expected turnaround time under constant price and quality-of-service conditions.[30] Such a relationship, called the *user demand function,* is represented in general form in Figure 6. Average demand over a given period is a nonincreasing function of expected turnaround time, where μ is the mean processing time of jobs run during that period.

Turnaround Time as a Function of Demand

Since the capacity of the internal computing facility is assumed to be fixed throughout the period, it is clear from queueing-theoretic considerations that the higher the average demand during the period, the greater the congestion in the system, and the longer the average expected turnaround time. The precise functional relationship depends on the sequencing rules and the parameters of the arrival and service systems. In the case of random arrivals, exponentially distributed service times, and a first-come-first-served queueing discipline, the form of the function—which will be called the *congestion delay function*—is as shown in Figure 7. A similar curve, relating the expected turnaround to the average demand in a given period, may be obtained under a variety of system assumptions.[31] Again, μ is the mean processing time.

Other characteristics of the turnaround-time distribution, such as

---

[30]C. P. Bourne, G. D. Peterson, B. Lefkowitz, and D. Ford. "Requirements, Criteria, and Measures of Performance of Information Storage and Retrieval Systems." Final report to the National Science Foundation, Stanford Research Institute Project 3741. December 1961. Unpublished.

[31]See W. S. Vickrey, "Congestion Theory and Transport Investment," *American Economic Review, 59*:251–260, May 1969, for a similar formulation in transportation, in which congestion delay is related to traffic volume.

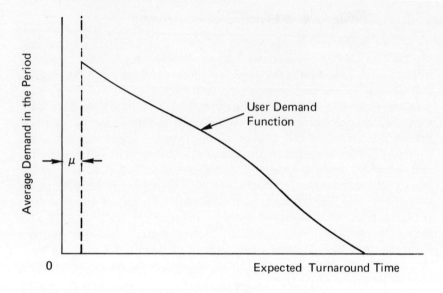

Figure 6   Average demand as a function of expected turnaround time.

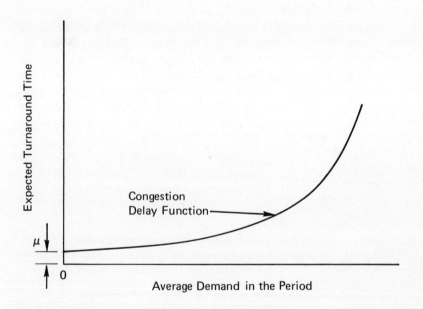

Figure 7   Expected turnaround time as a function of average demand.

variance, skewness, and upper confidence bounds, also may be related to the average demand.

The Equilibrating Process

If the analysis is limited to single variable functions (as in Figures 6 and 7) by considering average demand and expected turnaround time only, the stability of the system may be examined graphically.

A typical interaction, if such a feedback loop were invoked explicitly, would proceed as follows: Users receive an estimate of the expected turnaround time from the computer center, based on the administrator's prediction of demand and determination of turnaround from the congestion delay function.[32] Acting in a manner corresponding to the user demand function, users respond with a specific demand; this demand information is then resubmitted to the computer center. If the demand is different from the initial estimate, the administrator recalculates the turnaround time, and the new turnaround time is resubmitted to the users. This cycle continues until the average demand proffered by users to the computer center corresponds to the turnaround time that was presented to the users by the computer center on the previous iteration, indicating that a stable equilibrium point has been reached. A flow diagram of this process is shown in Figure 8. At equilibrium, the users submit that level of demand which produces the expected turnaround that itself induces the same demand level.

The next question is: Under what conditions will the system converge to a stable equilibrium?

The Cobweb Diagram

The conditions for stability will be discussed using an analog to the *dynamic cobweb* of demand economics.[33] The user demand and congestion delay functions can be superimposed on one graph, as indicated in Figure 9. The axes of the congestion delay function are rotated through a right angle to conform with the axes of the user demand function. In this way, both the users' and the computer

---

[32]The congestion delay function can be determined empirically, using historical values of demand (number of jobs, CPU utilization, and so on) and the turnaround experienced at these demand levels. The demand must be converted to a single measure, such as processing time, for this approach.

[33]For a description of the economic application of the dynamic cobweb, see P. A. Samuelson, *Economics,* 10th Edition, New York, McGraw-Hill, 1976, pp. 405–407.

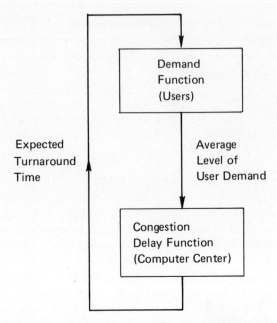

Figure 8   The demand/turnaround feedback loop.

center's responses may be compared directly. For example, if the computer center administrator estimates an average level of demand for the period of OA (see Figure 9), the expected turnaround time, from the congestion delay function, is OM.[34] The users then are informed that the turnaround time will be OM and they submit a demand, based on the user demand function, of OB. Since OB is different from OA, the computer center will revise its estimate of turnaround to ON. This process may converge to a stable equilibrium, diverge, or remain in persistent oscillation. The point of equilibrium is at the intersection of the two curves in Figure 9.

The behavior of the system depends on the relative slopes of the two curves, as shown in the three cases illustrated in Figure 10. Figure 10(a) shows convergence to equilibrium, which occurs if the slope of the congestion delay curve is greater than the absolute value of the slope of the user demand curve within the relevant range of demand and turnaround. In Figure 10(b), the curves are related in such a manner that the cycle returns to its starting point on the congestion delay function. This is persistent oscillation, neither converging nor diverging. It should be noted that the occurrence of persistent oscillations may appear as a result of the magnitude of the starting point (a turnaround of T_1 in this case). It is not necessary for the curves to be of constant gradient at all points for oscillatory behavior. A different

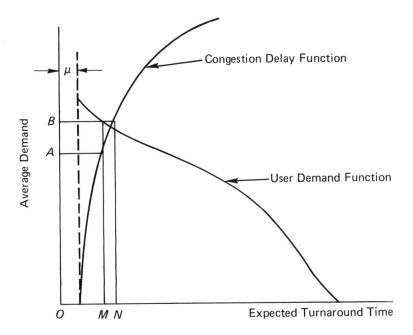

Figure 9   The "cobweb" diagram.

starting point might result in either a converging or diverging system, depending on the relative slopes of the curves. In Figure 10(c), the relative slopes of the curves are the reverse of Figure 10(a), with the process diverging, and the system is unstable.

The equilibrium point can be readily obtained using analytical methods if the curves in Figures 6 and 7 can be defined by continuous equations. If D is user demand, T is turnaround time, and μ is the mean processing time, the curve in Figure 6 can be expressed as:

$$D = \hat{D} - f_1(T - \mu), \qquad (1)$$

where $\hat{D}$ is the maximum user demand occurring when $T = \mu$ (i.e., when turnaround time equals processing time and queueing time is zero) and f_1 is some function that describes how the user demand falls as turnaround time increases. The curve in Figure 7 is given by:

$$T = \mu + f_2(D), \qquad (2)$$

---

[34]The user demand is typically expressed in time units, although the particular measure (e.g., CPU time, total processing time) will depend on the specific installation under consideration and the characteristics of the jobs.

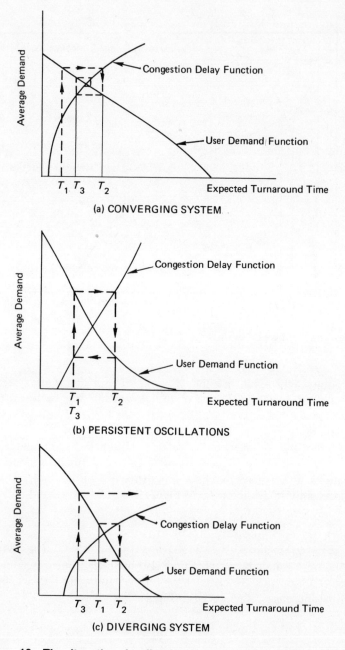

(a) CONVERGING SYSTEM

(b) PERSISTENT OSCILLATIONS

(c) DIVERGING SYSTEM

Figure 10   The iterative feedback process under various functional forms.

where f_2 is a function describing the increase in queueing time resulting from heavier demand. Substituting (2) into (1) gives:

$$D = \hat{D} - f_1[\mu + f_2(D) - \mu];$$

that is,

$$D = \hat{D} - f_1[f_2(D)]. \tag{3}$$

The equilibrium demand, D_E, is obtained by solving (3) for D, and the corresponding equilibrium turnaround time, T_E, is calculated by substituting D_E in (2).

A simple example will illustrate the procedure.

Let $\qquad\qquad\qquad D = 10.0 - 2.0(T - 2.0)$
and $\qquad\qquad\qquad T = 2.0 + 0.5D.$

This gives

$$D_E = 10.0 - 2.0(2.0 + 0.5D_E - 2.0),$$

which simplifies to

$$D_E = 10.0 - D_E.$$

Therefore, $\qquad\qquad D_E = 5.0$
and $\qquad\qquad\qquad T_E = 2.0 + (0.5 \times 5.0)$
$\qquad\qquad\qquad\qquad = 4.5$

Equilibrium occurs at a demand of 5.0 units, for which the average turnaround time is 4.5 time units.

The Use of "False" Responses

By recording the first three turnaround times of the process (shown as T_1, T_2, and T_3 in Figure 10), the computer center may categorize the particular system behavior into one of the three classes indicated, assuming that, within the area of interest, the curves do not change their relationships to each other. If the third turnaround time, T_3, falls within T_1 and T_2, as in Figure 10(a), the system is self-stabilizing and will converge to an equilibrium. When T_3 is equal to T_1, the system is of the persistent-oscillation type. If the computer center submits a false expected turnaround time to users of a magnitude greater than T_1 but less than T_2, the system will approach closer to the equilibrium point. This procedure could be repeated until either the equilibrium point is reached or the process changes to one of the other two categories. The system diverges if T_3 lies outside the interval $T_1 T_2$, as shown in Figure 10(c). The quoting of a false expected turnaround by the computer center also may be applied here, as for the persistent-oscillation case, in order to induce users to reach equilibrium.

The system is considered to be in equilibrium when two successive turnaround times are equal. Table 6 depicts how the computer center can identify various feedback behaviors and what actions it can take to attain stable equilibrium.

The Parameters That Affect Stability

The aforesaid analysis is based on the relative slopes of the two curves in Figure 9. Since the user demand schedule represents the basic demand for computing, which is determined not only by the turnaround time but also by user budgets and price and priority rules, its form may be changed by manipulating these controls. The congestion delay schedule, on the other hand, is derived from the characteristics of the queueing system. For example, increasing the capacity and speed of the computer facility extends the region of low-expected turnaround, such as in Figure 10(a) compared to Figure 10(c), where the latter represents a smaller capacity machine. This comparison implies that larger, faster, lightly loaded computers are more likely to have a converging feedback process than smaller systems for the same user demand function. Conversely, the process is more likely to be

Table 6   Stabilization Action for Various Feedback System Behaviors

Observation	Inference	Stabilizing Action by Computer Center
$\begin{cases} T_2 > T_1 \\ \text{or} \\ T_1 > T_2 \end{cases}$ and $T_3 = T_1$	Persistent oscillation	Quote false T between T_1 and T_2
$\{T_1 < T_3 < T_2\}$ or $\{T_1 > T_3 > T_2\}$	Convergence	No action—self-stabilizing system
$\{T_2 > T_1 \text{ and } T_3 < T_1\}$ or $\{T_1 > T_2 \text{ and } T_1 < T_3\}$	Divergence	Quote false T between T_1 and T_2
$T_{i+1} = T_i, i = 1, 2, \dots$	Equilibrium	No action

unstable for a heavily loaded system with users whose demand levels are very sensitive to turnaround time.

Extensions to the Computer Usage Allocation Model

The control model contains a number of simplifying assumptions to facilitate a graphical presentation. For example, it is a static model that does not consider changes in the demand and delay functions over time. Demand not only responds to turnaround time within a given time interval, it also varies with time of day, day of week, month, season, and so on. Thus, the same turnaround response may produce various levels of demands at different times, resulting in perhaps a shift, or a change in shape, of the user demand function. By noting such changes, the computer center can respond to the dynamic nature of demand and avoid the danger of applying an outdated cobweb diagram.

The congestion delay function depends on the speed and capacity of the computer. Any change in the computer hardware or system software that alters the effective speed or capacity of the system will result in a modification of the congestion delay function. Also, different user types may be affected by different delay functions: For example, if several priority classifications exist, each will present a different expected delay schedule to users, with higher priority jobs having shorter expected delays for a given demand level for that priority. This can be represented by a series of curves, each of similar shape to that shown in Figure 7, one for each priority.

The Economic Basis for Iterating

Since the organization will incur operating costs from the feedback process, the iterative procedure is justified on economic grounds only if it results in savings that are at least as great as the costs. The savings arise from increases in the total net value of jobs processed, which occurs when users experience a turnaround time close to the expected time. If turnaround is greater than anticipated, users may submit some jobs that have negative net value at the actual turnaround. If the turnaround is less than expected, users may refrain from submitting some jobs that would have produced a positive net value at the actual turnaround, but which have a negative net value at the expected turnaround.

SUMMARY

A computer usage allocation model was developed and used to examine the effects of prices, budgets, and priority rules as control measures. The stability of such a model was considered, and a number of strategies were suggested to recognize and counter undesirable features of the iterative process through which demand and turnaround time interact.

PART II

4 COSTS AND VALUES

Costs can accrue to the computing system either from the actual expenditure of economic resources (e.g., money or time) or through the loss in economic value of resources (e.g., from delays or unreliable service). A cost saving may be considered as a value increase when out-of-pocket expenses are not reduced and effectiveness is increased. In this chapter, the following aspects of costs and values (or benefits) are examined:

1. Costs attributable to the computing system
2. Values accruing to various parts of the organization from use of the computing system[1]
3. The relationship between the value of a job and various system characteristics

COST CONSIDERATIONS

There are two types of costs germane to the allocation of computing resources:

1. Actual cash outlays subject to the total computing budget constraint

[1]See J. L. King and E. L. Schrems, "Cost-Benefit Analysis in Information Systems Development and Operation," *ACM Computing Surveys, 10*:19–34, March 1978. King

2. Opportunity costs, in the form of reductions in values of jobs, that are not constrained by the budget[2]

Cash Outlays

In the computing allocation model postulated in this book, the funds of the computing budget may be spent on the installation and operation of an internal computer center and/or the services of external computing organizations should they be available. The actual amount of money assigned to each depends on knowledge of the optimal allocation of resources among the available choices. In a deterministic model, it is possible, though not usually simple, to arrive at a single configuration that is at least as satisfactory as any other known arrangement. In the probabilistic case, the best system configuration may be determined using expected values of the model variables; in retrospect, this approach may prove to be other than the best. The allocation of overhead costs presupposes a knowledge of the "correct organization for the firm."[3]

In practice, the organization must try to predict the user demand for computer services over the decision period and, using these *ex ante* estimates, must attempt to set up a system that will optimize some objective function within given constraints of resources. This type of analysis has been well documented, mainly with regard to the establishment of the best internal computing facility.[4,5] The usual approach is to establish some criterion: choose the system that will produce the highest output per unit cost, subject to a budget constraint; or choose the system for which the marginal value of the output is equal to the marginal cost, assuming that this gives a *maximum* net value or profit. In practice, a combination of both criteria is used; that is, the organization attempts to obtain the most effective system within the

---

and Schrems include benefits of the computerized systems and both computing and noncomputing costs. Examples of the latter are project-related costs, which, in the control model, are deducted from the value of the job prior to analysis. See also John B. B. Aris, "Quantifying the Costs and Benefits of Computer Projects," in: *Economics of Informatics*, edited by A. B. Frielink, Amsterdam, Elsevier/North-Holland, 1975, pp. 15–24.

[2]Value-related concepts are considered later in this chapter.

[3]C. W. Churchman. *Prediction and Optimal Decision*. Englewood Cliffs, N.J., Prentice-Hall, 1961, p. 51.

[4]A. B. Frielink, ed. *Economics of Automatic Data Processing*. Amsterdam, Elsevier/ North-Holland, 1965.

[5]W. F. Sharpe. *The Economics of Computers*. New York, Columbia University Press, 1969.

given budget, since the budget is estimated on the basis of the level of output that will optimize the overall operation of the organization.

The computer center's operating costs are similar to those Rothenberg attributes to an information retrieval system:[6]

1. Initial costs (e.g., system design and development)
2. Fixed costs (e.g., rent)
3. Operating costs (e.g., personnel supplies, maintenance)

Smidt states that an important characteristic of computer systems is that "there is a high ratio of fixed to variable costs in supplying computer services";[7] he assumes that the short-term marginal costs of running a job are zero. This may be true for an internal computer center but, in the longer term, many costs can be varied widely relative to the demand for services.

In contrast, the use of external computer services may involve negligible fixed costs, with the major cost component being related to the level of usage. This would occur if the use of some type of computer utility were envisaged. The utility might charge a fixed access price per job plus a given rate per unit of computing time, to which charges for additional services might be added. The specific relationship between pricing rules and demand will be affected by the market in computing services: If the market is perfectly competitive, that is, when there is a large number of suppliers and no single customer dominating the market, then the buying organization is confronted with a set of pricing rules that are independent of his demand. On the other hand, if the organization is a monopsonist, it will be able to negotiate more favorable terms of trade. Thus, a variety of market-dependent supply functions are feasible.

The organization must choose some combination of internal and external demand that best fulfills the requirements of its users, subject to the budget constraint. If the constraint is binding, then an increase in external usage will lead to a reduction of funds spent on the internal computing facility, and vice versa. In general, computer systems "are subject to significant indivisibilities,"[8] so that changes in capacity occur in large increments; however, the costs of external services are

[6]D. H. Rothenberg. "An Efficiency Model and a Performance Function for an Information Retrieval System." Comparative Systems Laboratory Technical Report No. 13. Cleveland, Ohio, 1967. Unpublished.

[7]S. Smidt. "Flexible Pricing of Computer Services." *Management Science, 14*:B581–B600, June 1968.

[8]*Ibid.*, p. B581.

more likely to vary directly with the level of usage (although a fixed lower limit on usage may be specified by the external supplier). Examples of the allocation of computing funds to internal and external facilities are considered for specific system configurations in Chapter 5.

Opportunity Costs

Unlike cash outlays, opportunity costs do not appear on the organization's profit and loss statement and are not bound to any predetermined budget constraint. Nevertheless, they are real costs and must be considered when optimizing the resource allocation model.

Some opportunity costs are readily determined, and their magnitudes may be obtained implicitly from the accounting records. In some cases, the market mechanism will indicate the existence of opportunity costs. Some of the costs are incurred by individuals in the organization, and others arise through the model's indirect influence on individuals and organizations far removed from it. Some direct opportunity costs derive from:

1. Waiting for jobs to be returned from the computer
2. Uncertainty as to when the job actually will be processed and returned to the user

These costs may be considered as losses in value.

In his analysis of the design of a priority rule, Greenberger specifies the cost of delay as an inverse measure of system performance.[9] The cost of delay may be termed as "disutility, penalty cost, loss of goodwill, opportunity cost, postponement of revenue, customer dissatisfaction, storage cost, poorness of service, or some equivalent" depending on the context.[10] Here, all such costs are defined as opportunity costs. Some writers are more specific in their treatment of waiting costs. Huskey distinguishes three types of computer users in a university environment:[11]

1. Students in classes who are attempting assigned problems

[9]M. Greenberger. "The Priority Problem and Computer Time Sharing." *Management Science, 12*:888–906, July 1966.
[10]*Ibid.*
[11]H. D. Huskey. "Economics of On-line and Batch Processing Computing in a University." In: *Economics of Automatic Data Processing,* pp. 340–345.

2. Staff and students who are attempting some computer problems as part of weekly tasks

3. Advanced graduate students and staff engaged in research who are spending all their time on computing

He asserts that students and staff in the first two categories may be able to tolerate fairly lengthy turnaround times relative to those of the third category, since the former may use the time spent waiting in accomplishing other tasks. Those in the third category, engaged full-time in computing, may be unable to do productive work while waiting; if high waiting costs are to be avoided, rapid turnaround is required.

Mueller reports that a survey of an information retrieval system

indicated that once the need for information arises, the requester's productivity drops until the information is obtained. Some men working on a single job virtually stop altogether. Others, with several irons in the fire, proceed with another problem, but such efficient utilization of time is uncommon. . . . Typically, efficiency during waiting drops 25%.[12]

If the user is paid on an hourly basis, it is a simple matter to calculate the cost to the organization due to the drop in efficiency. The cost of personal frustration due to waiting is much more difficult to assess.

These examples are typical of the current techniques for evaluating opportunity costs. The most significant opportunity cost may be the cost of time lost through delay; however, a more tangible cost is not necessarily more critical. Some less perceptible costs that may not be attributable to any specific aspect of the organization's operation, but which may have major impact, will be considered.

Less Tangible Opportunity Costs

If a computer center provides users with estimates of the expected value of some empirically derived turnaround-time distributions that prove to be optimistic, users will find that jobs have not been processed within the estimated time. Consequently, because the estimated turnaround time is not reliable, users will monitor the system more frequently. This results in an expenditure of time, which incurs a cost that is, to some extent, tangible and measurable. Furthermore, users will come to believe that the system, as a whole, is unreliable and

[12]M. W. Mueller. "Time, Cost, and Value Factors in Information Retrieval." In: *General Information Manual: Information Retrieval Systems Conference.* Brochure E20-8040. White Plains, N.Y., International Business Machines Corporation, 1960.

may not use it even when it might yield considerable real cost savings. Such costs are difficult to detect and measure.

The quality of computer services, either real or imagined, can have a significant effect on the actual and potential demand by current and prospective users. It has been shown that:

1. Features of the turnaround-time distribution, other than the expected value (e.g., variance), may affect the opportunity costs of the organization.

2. The opportunity costs accruing from these features of turnaround-time distribution may include costs resulting from the loss of potentially profitable jobs, as well as the specific waiting costs for known jobs.

The latter concept was expressed in a report prepared by the Woods Hole Oceanographic Institution:

There are more subtle effects of the present computer's limitations and these are harder to evaluate than the cost and inconvenience of purchasing outside time. These are the projects which are never started and the scientists who do not accept employment here. It is clear from interviews and studies that the lack of adequate computer facilities has been a factor in decisions not to initiate some research projects and in decisions not to join the research staff at the Woods Hole Oceanographic Institution.[13]

An article on the computer society in *Time* stated that "educational analysts report that high school students are increasingly choosing colleges on the basis of their computer facilities."[14]

Although such opportunity costs are extremely elusive and virtually impossible to measure, they can be of great importance and should not be ignored. For example, in a research center environment, the loss of a large contract could be detrimental to the economic viability of the entire organization; in academia, the failure to attract high-quality students and faculty could harm a college's reputation. The quality of education and research also can be influenced by the service level and availability of computer resources, both directly, since good computer support enables good work, and indirectly, due to the attractiveness of an excellent computer center to high-quality individuals.

In business, the quality of the computer function can have significant

[13]"Proposal to the National Science Foundation Office of Computing Activities for Support of New Facilities in the Information Processing Center." Woods Hole, Mass., Woods Hole Oceanographic Institution, January 1968, p. 14. Unpublished.
[14]"The Computer Society—Living: Pushbutton Power." *Time, 111*(8):46–49, February 20, 1978.

bearing on the competitive edge of an organization, particularly in service industries (such as banking, credit card, securities, and insurance firms) and large retail businesses (such as department stores and mail-order companies) where customers are exposed directly to the vagaries of the computer. Errors in billing, for example, can cause substantial financial losses, including loss of irate customers to competitors. Long customer waiting times at department store registers, bank windows, and airline reservation counters due to system failures or slow responses can have adverse effects on business.

Another important aspect of the quality of computer services is the availability of the services in times of accidental or sabotaged destruction of part or all of the computer center. The ability of an organization to survive such a catastrophe depends on contingency plans and backup facilities and the importance of the computer to the continuing operation of the organization. The amount spent on backup facilities should be related to the value of the work lost when the computer is not operating. The costs of the physical plant and of developing computer programs should be assessed; then, the physical equipment should be insured and copies of important programs should be made. FitzGerald suggests that management determine the cost of the total, direct loss of an asset and proposes a risk-analysis technique for evaluating contingency situations ranging from the loss of a communications message to a major disaster.[15] The opportunity costs of a computer unavailable for a short or long period can far outweigh the costs of the equipment, software, or personnel involved. Through the use of the value functions, introduced in the next section, a precise assessment of the cost of delayed operations or loss of the processing facility can be made, since the costly effect of delays on the value of jobs processed is the same whether the delay is caused by other jobs in the system, lack of sufficient capacity, or a fire or power failure in the computer room.

VALUE CONSIDERATIONS

The previous section illustrated how increases in opportunity costs may be considered as equivalent to reductions in value. Values may be expressed in monetary units and represented on the profit and loss statements of organizations if they are closely related to revenues. Other values, such as goodwill or reputation, may be less tangible. Two types of values pertinent to the control model will be

[15]J. FitzGerald. "EDP Risk for Contingency Planning." *EDPACS*, 6:1–8, August 1978.

discussed: those that are readily accessible and to some extent measurable and those that are elusive.

Value and Revenue

Sharpe defines *gross value* as the maximum amount (in dollars) that someone is willing to pay in order to obtain something, and *net value* as gross value minus cost.[16] Singer, Kanter, and Moore indicate that, if someone buys something for a given amount, then the buyer derives at least as much satisfaction from the object purchased as derived from the quantity of money paid.[17] Although this approach reduces value to a common measure (money), it does not determine the value of the money to either the buyer or the seller. When an organization sells its output and receives revenue, the value of this output to the organization may be assumed to be equal to the revenue received.[18] The value of the output to the buyer is equal to or greater than the buyer's value of the price paid—any positive difference between the former and the latter is termed *consumer surplus*.

Value and Cost Savings

Value usually is related to benefits or cost savings.[19] If there are two methods of achieving exactly the same goal but one costs more than the other (at market prices), the selection of the cheaper method results in a cost saving. Similarly, if two methods cost the same in actual cash outlay but one is twice as fast as the other, then the cost of waiting, if significant, will be reduced. This also results in a cost saving. Such savings represent real increases in value and may be regarded as *components* of a gross value figure. Brenner shows, however, that cost minimization does not necessarily lead to net value maximization and that, by neglecting the value aspects of information and by concentrating on costs only, a situation of diminishing returns may be reached in which reductions in cost accompany reductions in

[16]W. F. Sharpe. *Economics of Computers*, p. 11.

[17]N. Singer, H. Kanter, and A. Moore. "Prices and the Allocation of Computer Time." In: *Proceedings of 1968 AFIPS Fall Joint Computer Conference, San Francisco.* Montvale, N.J., AFIPS Press, 1968, pp. 493–498.

[18]The organization may derive other benefits from the sale of its output, such as national recognition, in addition to revenue. Such benefits may not be measurable in money terms.

[19]D. N. Streeter. "Cost-Benefit Evaluation of Scientific Computing Services." *IBM Systems Journal, 11*:219–233, 1972.

total value.[20] Fisher also points out that both out-of-pocket expenses and opportunity costs must be considered in the evaluation of computer systems.[21] A major opportunity cost, discussed by Marchand, is the inconvenience and delay one job causes all other affected jobs.[22] This will be examined when the impact of specifying value for different constituencies within the organization is analyzed later in this chapter.

The Measurement of Value

Since the control model does not have an open market for the computer output, it is not possible to establish even the lower limit of value to buyers, as may be obtained when a price mechanism is in operation. Cost savings, therefore, must be examined to estimate some of the components of value. Mueller suggests the following three methods for estimating the value of a computerized retrieval of information:

1. Estimate the average cost of retrieving a typical report stored in the system. Obtain the average number of retrievals per report. Calculate the average cost per retrieval.
2. Compare the cost of a retrieval with the cost of alternative methods of obtaining the same information.
3. By means of a questionnaire, find out how much "engineering time" was saved by each retrieval. Given the cost to the organization of engineering time (i.e., the wage rate), calculate the dollar value of the engineering time saved as a result of obtaining the information in the retrieved report.[23]

Mueller then compares the second and third methods as equivalent measures of value. The first measure is dismissed as a first approximation. The second and third measures are *different value components,* and their closeness in magnitude is purely coincidental. According to the specification of costs and values in this book, the first method is a cash outlay, the second is a cost saving, and the third is an opportunity cost reduction. The average cost of retrieving the stored report must

[20]J. R. Brenner. "Toward a Value Theory of Information." In: *Economics of Automatic Data Processing,* pp. 22–32.
[21]G. H. Fisher. *Cost Considerations in Systems Analysis.* New York, Elsevier, 1971, pp. 24–63.
[22]M. Marchand. "Priority Pricing with Application to Time-Shared Computers." In: *Proceedings of 1968 AFIPS Fall Joint Computer Conference,* pp. 511–519.
[23]M. W. Mueller. "Time, Cost, and Value Factors."

be considered in choosing between a given retrieval method for obtaining the information and other available methods; however, if the report has to be retrieved irrespective of whether or not the information retrieval system operates, then this cost is not relevant to the value aspects of system evaluation. Consequently, only that part of the report retrieval cost that is directly attributable to the particular information retrieval system should be considered in the analysis. The comparison of costs of various means of obtaining the same information also is used in the investment decision for selecting the best way of obtaining the information, but it is not directly relevant to the *value* of the retrieval. Only the third measure agrees with the definition of value used in the model. The organization should be willing to pay up to but not more than the dollar savings of a retrieval. If the difference in time saved by having the information available from the retrieval is the only benefit of the system, then that is the gross value of the retrieval. The actual cash outlay assignable to the retrieval and such opportunity costs as the loss of efficiency during waiting must be deducted from the gross value. The remainder is the net value of the retrieval.

If the net value is less than or equal to zero, then the retrieval should not take place; if the total net value of all retrievals is negative, then the system should not be established. The apparent savings (gross value) of a system may be less than the total costs, yet management may feel that the project is still worthwhile for intangible reasons. Such reasons may be, in fact, an expression of the intangible benefits that have not been included in the analysis—the "business intuition" of entrepreneurs may be their attempt to estimate the intangible costs and values.

Whereas Mueller suggests three methods for estimating value of computerized information retrieval that depend on the cost of retrieval and time savings,[24] Huskey relates the value of computer jobs specifically to the type of use and classifies use according to the dependency of users on the computer.[25] Streeter considers both system and user costs in his development of priority assignments.[26]

Consequently, there are two basic approaches to the measurement of value. One approach deals mainly with the classification of users and then estimates value based on the characteristics of the user

[24]*Ibid*.

[25]H. D. Huskey. "Economics of On-line and Batch Processing."

[26]D. N. Streeter. "Productivity of Computer-Dependent Workers." *IBM Systems Journal, 14*(3):292–305, 1975.

categories;[27] the other approach attempts to develop explicit relationships between waiting time and value loss.[28] The latter relationships are exemplified by the value hill concept that will be introduced in Chapter 6.

Value to Whom?

It has been implicitly assumed that values and costs are relevant only to the extent that they affect the organization and that the costs and values of individuals within the organization are considered only if they directly affect the organization itself.[29] This approach is acceptable if:

1. The objective is to maximize the net value of computing to the organization.
2. The organization controls all the actions of the individuals within it that pertain to this objective.

Sharpe points out that, for the net value maximization approach to be meaningful, "both total value and total cost must be measured in a manner relevant for the decision-maker. . . . The total value must be the total value *to him,* as must total cost. However, in some cases total value (or cost) may be the value (cost) to someone else as well."[30]

In his analysis of priority-pricing systems, Marchand states that "at the optimum, the social utility of an additional job should compensate the social disutility that its presence is causing to the users of the facility."[31] The social utility of the marginal job is equivalent to its private cost if "the incomes are optimally distributed among the individuals."[32] In other words, in the context of the control model, the optimal allocation of user budgets is necessary for the marginal

[27]See H. D. Huskey, "Economics of On-line and Batch Processing"; and D. N. Streeter, "Productivity."

[28]C. P. Bourne, G. D. Peterson, B. Lefkowitz, and D. Ford, "Requirements, Criteria, and Measures of Performance of Information Storage and Retrieval Systems," final report to the National Science Foundation, Stanford Research Institute Project 3741, December 1961, unpublished; and R. G. Cassidy, M. J. L. Kirby, and W. M. Raike, "Efficient Distribution of Resources Through Three Levels of Government," *Management Science, 17*:B462–B473, 1971.

[29]See also A. D. J. Flowerdew and C. M. F. Whitehead, "Measuring the Benefits of Scientific and Technical Information," in: *Economics of Informatics,* pp. 119–128.

[30]W. F. Sharpe. *Economics of Computers,* p. 61.

[31]M. Marchand. "Priority Pricing," p. 511.

[32]*Ibid.*

analysis of jobs to be applicable. It should be noted that Sharpe examines the maximizing of the net value of computing to the organization, whereas Marchand deals with optimization of a user-oriented objective function. Smidt, who assumes that "a dollar is equally valuable to all computer users,"[33] also has stated that the goals of users are consistent with those of the organization.[34]

The problem of determining the utilities of costs and values to the organization and its employees generally is removed from consideration. If a pricing mechanism is used as the effective allocative device, then it is *assumed* that the market, combined with an effective income allocation method, will operate to enable basic economic analysis to be used meaningfully. Little or no attempt has been made, by those proposing economic models for the allocation of computer resources via pricing and budgets, to indicate practical methods of measuring value and evaluating the effects of pricing and budgets on the inherent value of computing. These questions are addressed to some degree in this book although, admittedly, much work on the subject remains to be done.

Bourne et al. surveyed a population of prospective users of an information retrieval system and obtained a relationship between the percentage of respondents willing to wait up to a given number of days to receive most relevant references and the maximum waiting time.[35] The latter is a measure of the delay that reduces net value of retrieval *to the user* to zero. While the study does not take the additional, and necessary, step of relating users' values to those of the organization, it does indicate that the use of questionnaires can give approximations to value components, which then may be used in constructing the overall picture. King and Bryant advocate a similar survey approach for document transfer systems.[36]

Multivariate Value Functions

In this book, it will be assumed that functions can be obtained that relate the value of jobs to such factors as the time at which the job is submitted, the expected value, variance, skewness and

[33]S. Smidt. "Flexible Pricing," p. B590.
[34]S. Smidt. "The Use of Hard and Soft Money Budgets, and Prices to Limit Demand for Centralized Computer Facility." In: *Proceedings of 1968 AFIPS Fall Joint Computer Conference,* pp. 499–509.
[35]C. P. Bourne et al. "Requirements, Criteria, and Measures."
[36]D. W. King and E. C. Bryant. *The Evaluation of Information Services and Products.* Washington, D.C., Information Resources Press, 1971, pp. 237–248.

upper confidence limits of the turnaround-time distribution, and the convenience of the input-output system. It is further assumed that the value function so obtained represents the utility of the jobs to central control, the user population, and the computer center.[37]

Users respond to the allocation-control system by submitting their jobs at a time that will lead to the maximization of the value of each of their jobs. Central control applies measures that will influence the number of jobs submitted and the times at which they are submitted for processing to lead to a maximization of an aggregate value function that is the sum of all the individual job value functions. The computer center sequences jobs that have arrived for processing with the goal of maximizing the sum of the value functions of the jobs processed in a given period.

SUMMARY

Those factors that affect the costs and values of jobs run have been considered. From this analysis, a job value function that will be used extensively in succeeding chapters was developed.

---

[37]It is more likely that the value function of a job will be different (i.e., display different parameter values and/or contain a different group of independent variables) for each of the organizational divisions; however, the optimization objectives of the divisions apply whether or not the value functions are common to all divisions.

5

THE CHOICE
AMONG COMPUTER
SERVICES

Determining what type of computing facility will best suit the needs of users is a dynamic process—both in terms of changing user requirements and an ever-increasing choice of available facilities. Figure 11 illustrates the typical selection process faced by users and their organizations. Computing requirements can be satisfied by facilities ranging from manual or calculator-assisted computation to a complex assortment of computing capabilities.

The selection process is self-limiting, to a major extent, by the specifications of the users' requirements. Some applications are not feasible with particular facilities if they are to be performed within time and cost constraints. For example, a simple arithmetic calculation required only occasionally but needed immediately would justify use of a desk calculator, but not of a large computer, even in a time-sharing mode. The analysis of the contents of a huge data base, on the other hand, would be greatly facilitated on a large mainframe computer, as would a highly complex mathematical analysis that must be repeated frequently. Previously uneconomic applications become feasible as new technological breakthroughs are made, such as the micro-processor, which has enabled the distribution of processing power throughout society.[1]

Consequently, changes in the selection process of computer services result from changes in demand (i.e., the need to automate new

[1]A. C. Kay. "Microelectronics and the Personal Computer." *Scientific American,* *237*:230–244, September 1977.

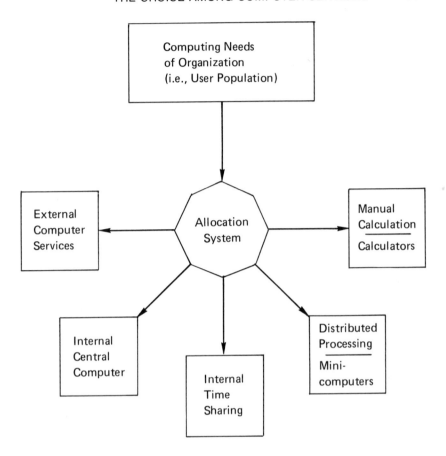

Figure 11 The computing facility selection process.

applications) and supply (i.e., technological and marketing advances). Of course, demand and supply are interactive, in that a new technology can make an application feasible, thereby creating additional demand for services.

It would be hard to imagine industries with large volumes of transactions, such as securities, airlines, communications, credit card, and banking, operating without the aid of computers. Many of these industries could not have grown to their present size without the efficient, accurate, and relatively inexpensive means of handling the tremendous transaction volumes that are provided by computers. In addition, many aspects of the services provided by such industries have become feasible only with recent technological advances in the computer field. Certainly, computerization has made possible the recent growth in the credit card business. Automatic bank tellers, which transfer funds electronically, allow bank customers to withdraw money from their accounts and conduct other types of transactions at any time of day. The convenience of electronic funds transfer undoubtedly generates an additional volume of transactions and attracts new customers. In the late 1960s, the lack of effective computer systems led to catastrophic operational problems in the U.S. securities industry when unprecedentedly high trading activities swamped brokerage houses. Subsequent improvement and increased use of computers has enabled the securities industry to handle large volumes of transactions without major operational problems.

In this chapter, the specific questions of whether or not an organization should supply computer services internally, should use external services, or should use a combination of internal and external services will be analyzed. The system, or combination of systems, yielding the highest net value should be selected. In addition, a pricing rule will be derived which will ensure that users, acting autonomously, submit jobs so as to attain the optimal internal/external mix.

ASSUMPTIONS

It is assumed that the direct cost of processing a job on an internal computer facility is negligible, so that only the fixed cost must be considered.[2] Consequently, the marginal cost of running a job internally is zero. The external facilities are assumed to charge a fixed rate per unit of demand that is independent of the organization's level of demand. The processing times of jobs are assumed to be the same for all the systems considered here; that is, the processors work at the same effective speed. Also, the value of a job run internally or externally is considered to be the same for the same turnaround time, which implies that all systems have comparable processing capabilities and produce effectively the same output for the same work done (i.e., they are not differentiable in terms of features, such as available compilers, utilities, and packages).

The queueing times experienced on external systems are regarded as being independent of the load placed on them by the jobs in question

[2]S. Smidt. "Flexible Pricing of Computer Services." *Management Science, 14*:B581–B600, June 1968.

and as being the same for all jobs. This is representative of a large capacity system with low utilization.

The assumption relating to internal turnaround times is varied with the three approaches described in this book, as follows:

1. Expected internal turnaround time is constant and independent of internal load (see "Selection on a Net Value Basis," p. 80)

2. Expected internal turnaround time varies with internal load but is constant throughout the time period (see Appendix B)

3. Actual internal turnaround time varies as the internal load changes over the time period (see Chapter 8)

The planning period of this analysis is the minimum period within which it is practical to set up, run, and close down a computer installation, since the resulting decision may involve the establishment of computer centers where none exist and/or the removal of existing facilities.

The computing budget of an organization is presumed to be divisible between expenditures on internal computing facilities and externally supplied services, if the latter are available.

The internal/external mix model that is presented in the following section assumes a single external facility; however, the analysis can be easily extended to a network of computers.[3] Furthermore, the assumption of a fixed external waiting time could be modified both in terms of relating it to load and having different waiting times for various job types or priorities.

THE OPTIMAL INTERNAL/EXTERNAL MIX

Selection on a Cost Basis

If the total expected demand in the given period is N units of processing time,[4] of which N_1 are processed internally and N_2 are processed externally, the relationship between the total cost of computing and the internal/external mix is as shown in Figure 12, where F

---

[3] W. J. Barr. *Cost Effective Analysis of Network Computers.* Springfield, Va., National Technical Information Service, 1972.

[4] At this macroplanning level, processing segments usually are considered to be major production applications and/or the aggregate of processing for an organizational unit, such as a department or division, rather than individual jobs. To facilitate presentation of the concepts, the general term *units of processing time* is used.

is the fixed cost of the internal facility and P is the price per unit of processing time for the external facilities. If all jobs are run internally, the total cost is F; if all jobs are processed externally, the cost is $P \times N$, since the internal facility would not be installed.

Under some circumstances, it is appropriate to select the optimal system solely on the basis of cost considerations.[5] In this case, if F is less than $P \times N$, all the jobs should be run internally; if F is greater than $P \times N$, no internal system should be acquired and all jobs should be run externally. If F and $P \times N$ are equal, *all* jobs should be run either internally or externally, but *not* a combination of both.

In reality, it is more likely that different sizes of internal computers could be used for different internal load situations.[6] As the number of internal jobs decreases, it is possible that smaller, cheaper computers could be used (as shown by the lower broken line in Figure 12), leading to an aggregate cost versus internal/external mix relationship (as shown by the upper broken saw-toothed line in Figure 12). In this case, the optimal job mix, on a cost-only basis, occurs at the lowest point of the saw-toothed line.

Selection on a Net Value Basis

The value functions of jobs are assumed to be insensitive to submission time within the given period (i.e., the user has no preference as to when he submits a job), but they do depend on the expected turnaround time. Clearly, the value of a job with respect to expected turnaround time is a monotonically nonincreasing function, such as that shown in Figure 13.[7] In this section, the optimal mix of internal and external computer services, assumed to be the mix at which the total net value of computing is a maximum (subject to an overall constraint on costs), will be determined.

The value of a job for an expected turnaround time can be obtained

[5]This would be valid if either (1) the expected turnaround time for internal and external services is the same at all times and there are no other significant differences in comparative service or (2) any differences in service between internal and external facilities do not affect the value functions of the jobs.

[6]Thomas E. Bell suggested adding the refinement of different computer sizes to the analysis after reviewing C. W. Axelrod, "The Effective Assignment of User Demand Among Computer Services," *CMG Transactions*, *15*:3-25–3-36, March 1977.

[7]See W. F. Sharpe, *The Economics of Computers*, New York, Columbia University Press, 1969, pp. 469–471. Sharpe describes a series of possible relationships between value and completion (or turnaround) time. Note that these relationships assume that the value is independent of the time at which the job is submitted—an assumption that is relaxed in Chapter 6.

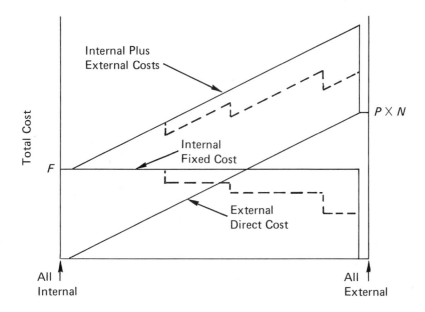

Source: Adapted from C. W. Axelrod. "The Effective Assignment of User Demand Among Computer Services." *CMG Transactions, 15*:3-27, March 1977. Reprinted by permission of The Computer Management Group, Inc.

Figure 12   Cost versus internal/external mix.

from the value function of Figure 13. It is assumed that the turnaround time of external services does not vary with the level of demand of the organization's users. The congestion delay function (Figure 7), however, indicates that the average demand of internally run jobs in the given period does influence the internal expected turnaround time. The average expected level of internal demand will be presumed to be well below the capacity of the internal facility, even when all N units are processed internally, so that the expected turnaround time does not vary appreciably with fluctuations in the demand level over the period as a whole. The more general case, in which the variation of turnaround with demand is a major factor, is analyzed in Appendix B.

If the internal and external average expected turnaround times are T_1 and T_2, respectively, and the value of the job is V_1 when it is run internally and V_2 when run externally, the latter values may be obtained for any job using the value function shown in Figure 13. If the internal turnaround time is greater than the external turnaround time

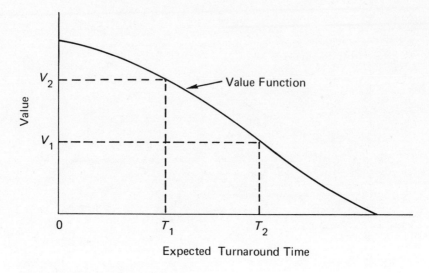

Source: C. W. Axelrod. "Effective Assignment," p. 3-27. Reprinted by permission of The Computer Management Group, Inc.

Figure 13   The relationship between the value of a job and the expected turnaround time.

for all jobs, then V_2 is always greater than or equal to V_1. If each job represents one unit of processing time and all jobs have identical value functions, the value of jobs run externally and internally for the full range of internal/external mix is as indicated in Figure 14(a). The total value of jobs for the range of mix is represented by the solid line in Figure 14(b). The dotted line in Figure 14(b) is the sum of the internal and external costs from Figure 12. By subtracting the total cost from the total value, the total net value curve of Figure 14(c) is obtained. The total net value is optimized in this case when all the jobs are run internally, since the net value of an all-internal decision, $(V_1 \times N) - F$, is greater than the net value of an all-external decision, $(V_2 \times N) - (P \times N)$.

Under the very restrictive assumption of identical jobs, the net value curve will always be a maximum at one extreme or the other, unless the two net values are equal. In the latter case, either selection is optimal, although a combination of internal and external processing is not.

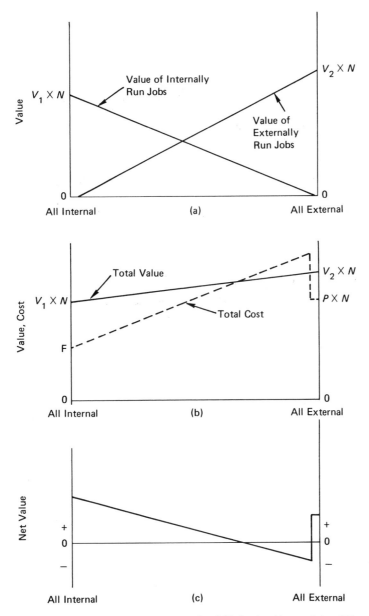

Source: C. W. Axelrod. "Effective Assignment," p. 3-28. Reprinted by permission of The Computer Management Group, Inc.

Figure 14   The net value as a function of the internal/external mix.

Different Job Value Functions

If it is no longer assumed that the value functions of all jobs are identical, the value of job i, when run internally and externally, can be represented as $V_{1,i}$ and $V_{2,i}$, respectively. D_i is the amount by which $V_{2,i}$ is greater than $V_{1,i}$. In the cases under consideration, D_i is always positive, although it may just as readily be negative.

Equal Value Differences

When the value functions of jobs are different but all the D_i are equal, the total value curve is a straight line, even though the respective values of internal/external combinations exhibit ranges that are shown in Figure 15 by the cigar-shaped envelopes. Consequently, the optimization conditions also are valid for this case. Figure 15 illustrates an example with five jobs.

Different Value Differences

When the D_i are different, the total value curve will be a cigar-shaped envelope (as shown in Figure 16). The envelope indicates the range of possible total values at any given mix of internal and external jobs. For example, if all the jobs are run externally, the total value is 27. If one job is run internally, the total value may be reduced by as little as zero, when job 3 is run internally, and by as much as 6 when job 4 is run internally. Thus, the total value may vary from 21 to 27 if one job is run internally and four are run externally. If this analysis is extended to all possible mixes, the envelope curve of Figure 16 is obtained.

The upper boundary of the envelope is called the *efficient bound* of total value. If it can be shown that it is optimal to run some jobs internally and the rest externally, then those jobs that combine to give a point on the efficient bound for the specific optimal mix should be selected. In Figure 16, the upper bound is expressed by the relationship: Total value $= 16 + 3N_2 - 2.5 \mid N_2 - 2.5 \mid^{2.5}$. This is a close approximation to the actual curve, obtained by trial-and-error methods. This relationship for the efficient bound is substituted into Figure 14(b) for the total value curve, and the mix that yields the maximum net value may be obtained as before.

In the example in Appendix B, the upward concavity of the efficient bound allows for a net value maximum to occur at some intermediate mix of internal and external processing. This phenomenon cannot occur when the total value function is linear.

Job No.	$V_{1,i}$	$V_{2,i}$	D_i
1	2	5	3
2	3	6	3
3	1	4	3
4	4	7	3
5	2	5	3
Total	12	27	

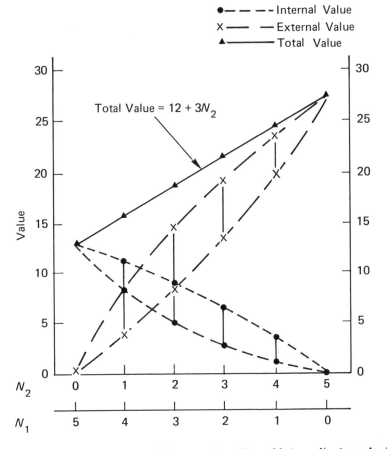

Figure 15   The total value of jobs as a function of internal/external mix for all equal D_i.

Job No.	$V_{1,i}$	$V_{2,i}$	D_i
1	3	5	2
2	2	6	4
3	4	4	0
4	1	7	6
5	2	5	3
Total	12	27	

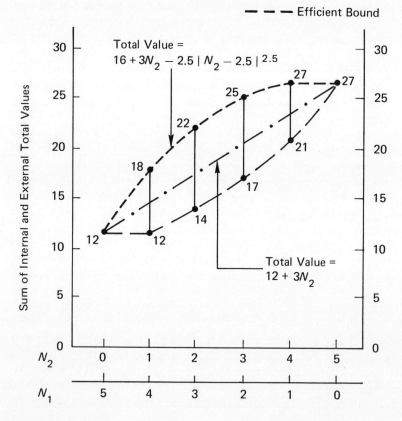

Figure 16   The total value of jobs as a function of internal/external mix for different D_i.

MARGINAL VALUE DIFFERENCE PRICING

The marginal value difference pricing rule induces individual users to submit, in any given period, those jobs that are to be run internally and those that are to be processed externally so as to maximize the total net value to the organization of the jobs. Central control performs the net value analysis described in the previous section and obtains the optimal combination of internal and external jobs. The solution is subject to net value maximization or the budget constraint, whichever is binding. In order to realize the optimal combination, central control may either issue separate, nontransferable budgets for internal and external use or direct users to distribute their jobs between internal and external facilities. The same objective may be achieved by using the marginal value difference pricing rule.

Since the price of external computer services is given, the objective of the rule is to set an internal price that will induce the desired selection by the user of those of his jobs that should be run internally. No specific information is given to the user other than the prices and turnaround times of both internal and external computing facilities.[8] The pricing rule is as follows: Select an internal price where the difference between the external price and the internal price is less than the smallest value difference, D_i, of any job i to be run externally and greater than the greatest value difference of any job to be run internally in the optimal combination.

This rule is illustrated using the example of Figure 16. Suppose that the five jobs in the exhibit represent the jobs of a single user and that central control determined that two of the user's jobs should be run externally and the remainder internally. In the general optimal solution, of the jobs with the highest value differences (in Figure 16, those jobs make up the efficient bound on the net value curve), two belong to the user in question. The job values listed in Figure 16 are repeated in Table 7.

According to the pricing rule, if the actual external price per job is 5, then the difference between the external and internal price should be between 3 and 4, giving a feasible internal price of 1.5. The user is assumed to subtract each price from the value and to decide whether to run the job internally or externally, based on which alternative generates the greater net value. The net value of job 1 is zero when run externally but its net value is 1.5 when run internally; accordingly, the

---

[8]It is assumed here that the users' job value functions are the same as those of the organization.

Table 7   The Selection of a Processing Facility

Job Number	External Value	Internal Value	Value Difference	Processing Facility
1	5	3	2	Internal
2	6	2	4	External
3	4	4	0	Internal
4	7	1	6	External
5	5	2	3	Internal

user concludes that the job should be run internally. The external net value of job 2 is 1 and its internal net value is 0.5, so job 2 is run externally, and so on. The resulting selection of a processing facility for each job is shown in the final column of Table 7. The selection of internal versus external computing does not depend on the absolute prices of each alternative but on the magnitude of the difference between internal and external prices.

6

MACROSEQUENCING: CONTROL OF THE LEVEL AND PATTERN OF DEMAND

The pricing mechanism developed in Chapter 5 was based on value functions that were related to the turnaround time—the actual clock time at which jobs are submitted for processing was not considered.[1] In this chapter, the concept of submission time is introduced into the value function analysis. First, it is assumed that external computer facilities are such that, if their turnaround times and pricing rules vary over time, they do so independently of the demand of internal users. Second, turnaround-time schedules of internal computer facilities may vary with clock time and are affected by the level and pattern of demand by internal users. Third, internal pricing, budgetary, and sequencing rules may be used by the organization to regulate the pattern of internal demand.

COMPONENTS OF THE DEMAND TIME SERIES

The demand for computer services generally varies over a period of time.[2] Specific components of the pattern of demand for

[1]In Chapter 5, the variance (and other characteristics) of the turnaround-time distribution was assumed to be independent of clock time. It is possible for the variance of turnaround time to fluctuate over time, just as the expected turnaround time can change. In addition, the relationship between the value of a job and the turnaround variance can change over time. For example, a user may be less willing to accept uncertainty (i.e., variance) the closer it gets to the job deadline.
[2]Some computer installations perform a single task or series of tasks that are known to have constant demand. An example would be an on-line computer controlling a

services, such as "trend," "cycle," "seasonal," and "irregular," are usually discernible.[3] Such analysis of time series facilitates the prediction of future demand patterns; however, these components are specified here to determine which are within the control of the organization and which are not.

1. *The Trend over the Lifetime of the System:* It frequently is contended that demand for the services of the internal computing facility by internal users is below "capacity" for some initial period, after which it becomes increasingly heavy until the system is overloaded and requires a larger facility to meet demand.[4] The increasing trend of computer usage over time, which may occur even when the organization is not experiencing any growth, may be attributed to a "learning effect" of both potential and current users. After the system becomes operable, there may be a lag before sufficient computer-operating personnel are acquired and trained and before potential users attain computing expertise. As users' knowledge increases, they usually discover new applications for the computer in their work. The upward trend might converge asymptotically to some ceiling, representing saturation of computer usage; however, the continual development of new applications would indicate a rising ceiling over time.

2. *Seasonal Variations:* Many organizations are subject to recurrent annual patterns of operation and, consequently, of computer service demand. Although it cannot be assumed that seasonality in one aspect of an organization's operation, such as sales, necessarily leads to sympathetic fluctuations in computing, certain patterns, such as heavy usage towards the end of a business reporting period or university semester and light demand during vacations or in the off-season, often appear.

---

production process in a manufacturing plant where the computer is devoted to one particular use that is scheduled by the single user.

[3]See Chapter 4 of R. G. Brown, *Smoothing, Forecasting and Prediction,* Englewood Cliffs, N.J., Prentice-Hall, 1963.

[4]The long-term changes in the demand pattern are cited as leading to undesirable resource allocation when average-cost pricing is in effect, since low initial demand results in high initial prices that discourage demand at a time when it should be encouraged, and high subsequent demand produces low prices that encourage demand in an already congested system. See H. Kanter, A. Moore, and N. Singer, "The Allocation of Computer Time by University Computer Centers," *Journal of Business, 41*:377, July 1968, and S. Smidt, "Flexible Pricing for Computer Services," *Management Science, 14*:B582, June 1968.

3. *Regular Requirements:* Certain uses of the computer are by nature periodic. For example, payrolls may be run weekly, bimonthly, monthly, or a combination of these schedules if employees are subject to different wage-receipt frequencies. Certain reports to management may have a fixed interval between successive runs.

4. *Weekly Variations:* If a five-day week is in effect for users, the submission of jobs will be relatively heavy on working days and light or nonexistent during weekends. If the computer is run weekends to absorb backlogs, it may be desirable to have a relatively heavy demand towards the end of the workweek that may be processed over the weekend.

5. *Daily Variations:* The fluctuations of demand throughout the day may follow a pattern of heavy demand during working hours that increases towards the end of the day, especially when the backlog is run at night.

6. *Random Variations:* In most computer installations, the demand within an hour or smaller interval probably does not conform to any discernible regular pattern. The facilities also will experience elements of demand that are not fully explained by an aggregation of individual components, such as trend and seasonal. This "irregular" component may affect the time series at any level (i.e., large contracts of random size that may arise occasionally at some random date, the submission of a test job on the spur of the moment, or a rerun).

The Control of Variations

Central control can use a number of measures to affect the pattern of demand. Some are direct rules (e.g., certain jobs may be restricted to given times of day, week, month, or year); some are less direct, leaving some discretionary power in the hands of users (e.g., a flexible budget-pricing scheme); while others combine direct and indirect means (e.g., a priority-pricing scheme may combine the restrictiveness of priorities with the flexibility of pricing).

In a typical system with demand information readily available to users, the demand pattern is self-regulating, because users are deterred by the high costs of waiting during a heavily congested period and are attracted by the rapid turnaround during periods of light demand.[5] If users are aware of the variations in demand, and hence in turnaround time, they will select that time of submission which will yield the

---

[5]A. B. Aroaz and H. B. Malmgren. "Congestion and Idle Capacity in an Economy." *Review of Economic Studies,* 28:202–211, June 1961.

greatest net value of the job.[6] The purpose of centrally imposed controls is to induce users to submit their jobs so as to maximize the overall net value to the organization of jobs submitted during a given period.

The Period of Effect of Controls

The effectiveness of a particular control on demand is closely related to the time interval over which the method is influential. An annually allotted fixed budget, for example, controls the annual level of demand but does not have any direct effect on seasonal variations. On the other hand, a perishable annual budget constrains total usage within fractions of the year. Because the user cannot transfer his budget from one subperiod to another, central control can manipulate seasonal fluctuations in demand. Budgetary control typically is long term, since it can be costly and inconvenient to vary budgets in the short term. Pricing rules *per se* also are not suitable for short-term change, whereas specific flexible pricing rules may be designed to respond dynamically to changes in the system.

MULTIDIMENSIONAL VALUE FUNCTIONS

The value of a job has been related to the first and higher moments of the turnaround-time distribution and other aspects of service. This concept is extended by postulating that the value of a job also is a function of the clock time at which it is submitted at the computer facility, T_s. It is assumed here that the expected turnaround time, ET_t, is the only significant factor, other than T_s, influencing the value of a job.[7]

The value of job i, submitted at clock time T_s, for which the expected turnaround time is ET_t, is given by $v_i(T_s, ET_t)$. The value of a particular job for all feasible submission times and all expected turnaround times may be shown on a two-dimensional graph of v_i (see Figure 17). The lines on the graph that represent loci of points of equal value are called *iso-value curves*. Such a contour diagram of v_i is called a *value hill*. As shown in Figure 17, the outermost curve represents the combinations

---

[6]This assumes rational behavior on the part of the user in that he responds so as to maximize his personal utility.

[7]The subsequent analysis is equally valid for value functions including more than the two independent variables used here; however, simplifying to two variables facilitates the analysis and permits a graphical presentation of the concepts.

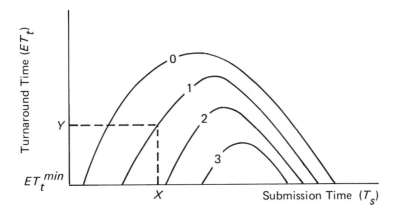

Source: C. W. Axelrod. "The Effective Use of Computer Resources." *Omega*, 4(3):323, August 1976. Reprinted by permission of Pergamon Press.

Figure 17   A value hill.

of submission and turnaround times that yield zero net value for that job (labeled 0 in the diagram). The other curves, labeled 1, 2, and so on, represent lines of successively higher values. If a job is submitted at time X and experiences a turnaround time of Y, the value attained is 1.

Figure 18(a) indicates the value hill of a job for which the value at the minimum expected turnaround time, ET_t^{min} (which usually is the expected processing time), gradually increases with time of submission, T_s, to a maximum at A and then gradually decreases to zero, as shown in the cross-sectional view along XX in Figure 18(b). Similarly, at any given T_s, for which the value of the job at ET_t^{min} is positive, the value gradually decreases with increasing ET_t, as shown in the cross-sectional view along YY in Figure 18(c). The value function with respect to ET_t is monotonically nonincreasing; however, at a given ET_t, the value of the job is not necessarily a nonincreasing function of T_s, as can be seen from the curve to the left of A in Figure 18(b).

The Derivation of a Value Hill

In this section, the relationship between the net value of a job and its submission time (i.e., time of day on a specific date) and expected turnaround time is examined. Although Sharpe related value to completion time (i.e., submission time plus turnaround time), he did

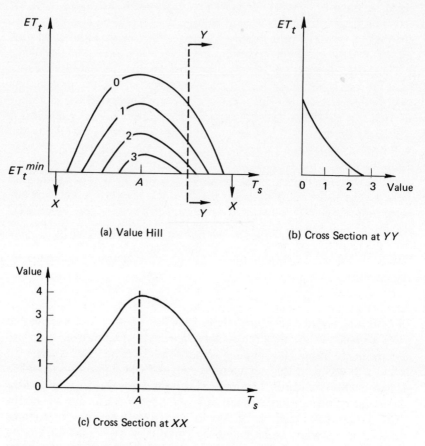

(a) Value Hill

(b) Cross Section at YY

(c) Cross Section at XX

Figure 18   Value hill with cross-sectional views.

not consider the variation of value with each of these two components of completion time.[8] It is contended here that a user may ascribe *different* values to the *same* completion time for a job *submitted at different times*. For example, an additional cost may be incurred for express delivery of input rather than normal delivery if the input data arrived late at the data preparation area and had to be run on a tight deadline, or perhaps the data preparation process could be speeded up by hiring additional people, buying more expensive equipment, or

[8]W. F. Sharpe. *The Economics of Computers.* New York, Columbia University Press, 1969, p. 470.

using an outside service. Also, the error rate might increase under the psychological pressure of a nearing deadline, resulting in costs due to the errors. As shown in Figure 19(a), efforts to have input submitted earlier usually will involve greater costs the earlier the input is needed.

Generally, the later a job completes processing, the less its value is likely to be, since costs of delay may be incurred and the information may be less useful. For instance, a computer-generated report that is needed at a periodic management meeting might have no value if it is not ready on time. If, however, it is known in advance that the report will not be available for the meeting, discussion of the report possibly could be postponed to a subsequent meeting, where it would still have some value, although perhaps not as much as for the earlier meeting. In general, the value of a job can be expected to vary with submission and turnaround times, as illustrated in Figure 19(b). Here the line labeled "value $= 3$" is flat up to submission time BB and then turns downward for later submission times. As the completion deadline for the job is approached, shorter and shorter turnaround times are needed to achieve the same job value.

Prior to BB, a turnaround time of P yields a value of 3 for all submission times, since completion will occur before the deadline. If the job is submitted at time Q, a turnaround time of R is required to yield a value of 3, due to the proximity of the deadline.

Subtracting the cost of input preparation (C_p) from the "value $= 3$" curve will produce the net value curve shown in Figure 19(c). The dotted curve in Figure 19(b) indicates the relationship between value and expected turnaround and submission times for "value $= 4$," which gives the net value contour shown in Figure 19(c) after subtraction of $C_p(T_s)$. The complete value hill, as shown in Figures 17 and 18, can be built up using the procedure illustrated in Figure 19. To the cost of input preparation in Figure 19(a) can be added other similar costs, such as transportation costs; however, opportunity costs, such as the cost of waiting, quality of service, and so on, produce changes in the value curve of Figure 19(b) and are not included in Figure 19(a). The cost of processing is not included at this point because it is a *decision variable* and not a component of the net value hill.

Different Value Hill Shapes

Some jobs may be highly sensitive to the time of submission. For example, it could be convenient for a user to submit a job at one time, but impractical to submit it either earlier or later. This might occur if a systems consultant who assists in submitting the program

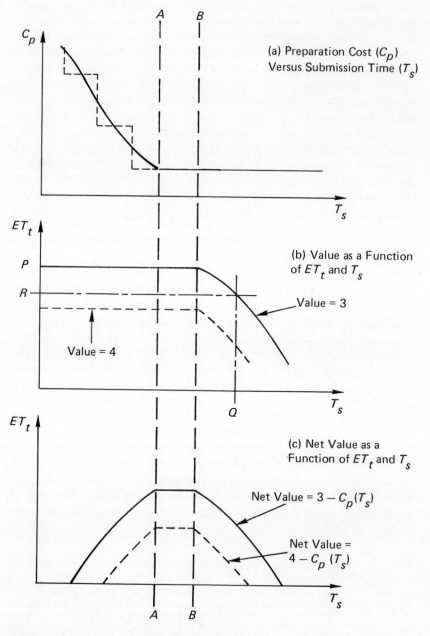

Figure 19   Derivation of the net value hill.

was available for a limited time only. The value hill for such a job may be as shown in Figure 20(a). The value of the job may or may not be sensitive to ET_t; in Figure 20(a), it is shown to be somewhat insensitive to ET_t, indicating that, although there are severe constraints as to when the job can be submitted, the time it takes for completion is relatively unimportant.

In Figure 20(b), the value of the job with respect to ET_t is shown as being virtually independent of the time of submission over a wide range. Such a situation was presumed to exist in Chapter 5, when the value schedules were assumed to be completely independent of T_s throughout the entire period. This form of value hill indicates that the primary cost is the cost of waiting and might be illustrative of a time-sharing environment, where the user is most sensitive to the response time of the system but also is relatively indifferent as to when he signs on to the system over a broad range of time.

Figure 20(c) illustrates the case of an absolute clock-time deadline or due date at B. The net value of the job is zero if it becomes available after processing later than time B (i.e., the sum of T_s and ET_t must not exceed completion time B for the job to have positive net value).

There are infinitely many possible iso-value curve configurations, although certain rules must be followed. The contours may touch, indicating an instantaneous drop in value, but they cannot cross, since the value functions are single-value types. A contour may not form a closed loop, since value functions are assumed to be monotonically nonincreasing in ET_t. If a job is completed earlier, the user can wait and pick it up later with no loss in value, assuming that there is no holding cost.[9]

THE MAXIMUM VALUE OF A JOB

It has been assumed that a user always behaves so as to maximize the net value of each of his jobs. The general value hill of Figure 21 and an exogenously determined ET_t schedule, $ABCDE$, expressed as a function of clock time, will now be considered. To maximize the job's net value, the user should submit the job at time T_s^*, which will yield a net value of approximately 3.3. The time at

[9]For an examination of the effect of a linear holding cost, see C. Lebon, "An Opportunity Costing Model for the Evaluation of Scheduling Rules," paper presented at the Operations Research Society of America/The Institute of Management Sciences Joint National Meeting, San Juan, Puerto Rico, October 1974.

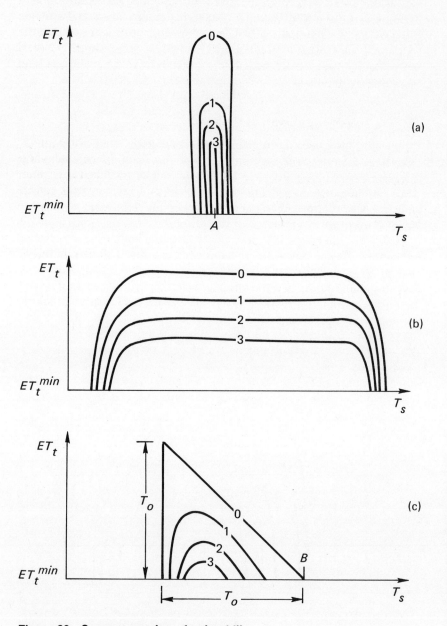

Figure 20   Some examples of value hills.

which the user submits his job and the size and type of the job may actually affect the ET_t schedule. If there are many users and any one job does not notably influence the system, it may be assumed that the individual user cannot affect the ET_t schedule significantly. Central control can adjust the ET_t schedule so as to obtain the maximum total net value by means of budgetary, pricing, and scheduling rules.

Self-regulation of Demand

The process by which a user, confronted with an ET_t schedule, submits a job at a time that provides the maximum net value suggests an iterative procedure, analogous to that described in Chapter 3 for obtaining an equilibrium schedule. In this case, central control presents users with an estimated ET_t schedule. The users respond to this ET_t schedule by stating their demand levels and the times at which jobs will be submitted. Central control then calculates a revised ET_t schedule based on the users' responses, and submits this to the users, and so on.

The stability of the iterative process depends on the form of the value functions of the jobs involved. If the jobs are predominantly of the type

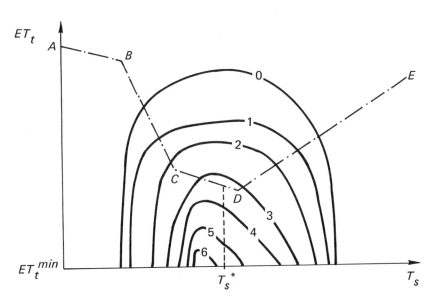

Figure 21   A general value hill cut by the ET_t schedule, *ABCDE*, giving a maximum value at point *D*.

with value functions that are highly sensitive to T_s, that is, similar to Figure 20(a), the iterative process will tend to converge more rapidly to an equilibrium, since the submission times of the jobs will not vary as much. Consequently, the major factor affecting the ET_t schedule in this case is the decision by users of whether or not to submit individual jobs. On the other hand, if most jobs' value functions are relatively insensitive to T_s, that is, similar to Figure 20(b), the iterative process will tend to converge less rapidly to an equilibrium, since the submission times will vary greatly in response to slight changes in the ET_t schedule. This behavior of the system is typified by the illustrative example of Appendix c.

A number of centrally imposed controls and their effects upon the system will be considered next.

The Effect of Peak-Load Pricing Rules on Demand

As stated earlier, a pricing rule must be considered in the context of the budgetary policy in effect. For example, if a user has a fixed budget for computing that is not transferable to another period, he will control his expenditures near the beginning of the period, based on his projected computer usage. Closer to the end of the budget period, the user may have a surplus of funds. He may respond to this situation by wasting the excess budget on jobs of little or no net value; however, this action imposes opportunity costs on other users. Conversely, if the user is short of funds due to an insufficient budget allocation, he may be restricted from running jobs of greater net value than his expenditure would indicate, thereby losing potential net benefits to the organization.

Figure 22(a) is similar to Figure 21 in that it shows a general value hill and ET_t schedule (AA'). The maximum net value at point A^* is attained when the user submits the job at time T_s^*. If a peak-load pricing rule, illustrated by Figure 22(b), is now introduced, the value hill takes on the form shown in Figure 22(c). This is derived by subtracting the price at any T_s from the value function of the job at the same T_s.

With the same ET_t schedule as in Figure 22(a), the maximum net value now occurs at A^{**}, giving the somewhat later optimal submission time of T_s^{**}, as shown in Figure 22(c). This has the effect of reducing the net value from approximately 2.7 at A^* in Figure 22(a) to approximately 1.9, which occurs at A^{**} in Figure 22(a). Since the pricing of internal services is not a cost recovery mechanism, the original value function, that is, that which has not been altered by the price schedule, is the one used to obtain the actual net value of a job. Although in this

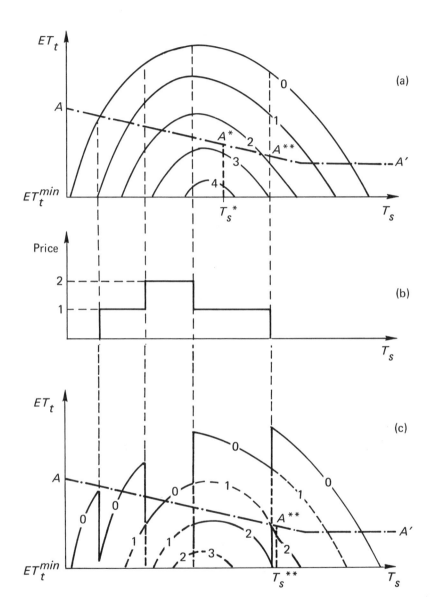

Figure 22   The effect of peak-load pricing on the time of submission.

example the net value is reduced, this need not mean a reduction in the total net value of all jobs run in the period if, as a result of the rule, the change in net value aggregated over all jobs is nonnegative.

The Effect of Microsequencing and Priority Rules

Peak-load pricing rules can have an effect on whether or not a job is submitted for service, since at some price levels the value hills may not intersect with the ET_t schedule (indicating zero net value for all T_s). Such jobs should not be processed. The pricing rules also affect the times at which the jobs are submitted. Microsequencing rules affect the values of jobs once they have been submitted; however, microsequencing will clearly influence whether or not a job is submitted if the rule is known to the user in advance. Many microsequencing disciplines have the effect of presenting different ET_t schedules for jobs with different characteristics, such as size, type, and priority. The user then makes his decisions and evaluations based on the ET_t schedule pertaining to jobs with the specific characteristics of the one he is submitting.

The fundamental difference between peak-load pricing rules and microsequencing rules is that the former alter the height and shape of the job value hill, whereas the latter influence the ET_t schedule and *not* the value hill.[10] Both types of rules may have an effect on whether or not a job should be submitted and the time at which it is submitted. The effect in any particular case will vary with the rules in operation and will depend on the form of the value function. Figure 23(a) shows the effect of two different priority rules: The ET_t schedule AA' is for low-priority jobs and BB' is the ET_t schedule for high-priority jobs. Changing the job from the lower to the higher priority results in a shift in submission time from T_s^A to T_s^B and an increase in value from 1.9 to 4.4.

The objective of any microsequencing rule is assumed to be the maximization of net value in the long run. Many microsequencing rules commonly examined by operations researchers, such as the shortest-job-first rule, presume that the value functions of jobs are independent of T_s. The minimization of average waiting time also is considered implicitly to be equivalent to net value maximization. Some rules, such as the c/t rule (see Chapter 7), are based on the minimization of

---

[10]Priority pricing affects both the value hill, through higher cost, and the ET_t schedule, through microsequencing.

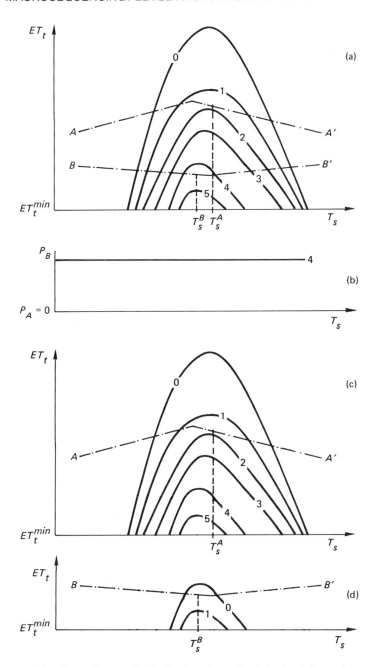

Figure 23 The effects of priority levels and related pricing rules on the value hill of a job and on the ET_t curve.

opportunity loss.[11] This is the inverse of performance measurement with respect to value.

To summarize, the effects of microsequencing rules usually are evaluated in terms of the shape of the ET_t schedule rather than in terms of value functions. The value aspects of the microsequencing of jobs will be considered in greater detail in Chapter 7, when the value implications of the more common rules are examined.

Priority-Pricing Schemes

Greenberger, for example, has asserted that priorities and prices are closely related in terms of their respective allocative effects.

Priorities and prices are related concepts. They each serve to allocate limited resources. A pricing-priority system makes the relationship explicit.[12]

Singer, Kanter, and Moore also suggest that

priorities are simply a surrogate set of prices which may in some instances work as well as a true price mechanism but will almost never be superior.[13]

In Figure 23, however, it is shown that priorities affect the ET_t schedule when higher priorities yield shorter ET_t and that pricing affects the shape of the value functions. The effect of superimposing the pricing scheme of Figure 23(b), in which the higher priority jobs are subjected to a price per job of P_B, as indicated in Figure 23(d), is to reduce the altitudes of the contours of the value hill. Under this particular priority-pricing scheme, the job has a maximum value of 1.7 for low priority and 4.4 for high priority. The price charged, P_B, causes the job to be run at low priority, since the net value price of running at the high priority is 0.4 compared to 1.7 for the low priority.

This example highlights a major difference between priorities and pricing not stated explicitly by other researchers: The effect of the pricing part of the rule on value is known with certainty, in that the price may be subtracted from the known value function. On the other hand, the effect of the priority rules on the ET_t schedules typically cannot be predetermined. Thus, the pricing mechanism has greater

---

[11]M. Greenberger. "The Priority Problem and Computer Time Sharing." *Management Science, 12*:888–906, July 1966.

[12]*Ibid.*, p. 905.

[13]N. Singer, H. Kanter, and A. Moore. "Prices and the Allocation of Computer Time." In: *Proceedings of 1968 AFIPS Fall Joint Computer Conference, San Francisco.* Montvale, N.J., AFIPS Press, 1968, pp. 493–498.

precision because its effect on each job can be evaluated, whereas priorities have a less well-determined effect.

Flexible Pricing and Microsequencing Rules

The aforementioned allocation rules are determined at the outset of the period and do not change in response to dynamic variations in the system. Flexible rules are defined as those that do respond dynamically to changes in the queue characteristics of the computer system, although the features of the rules are fully specified at the start of the scheduling period.

Smidt suggests two flexible rules in which the user can specify either the maximum price he wishes to pay (the maximum rate specified or MRS rule) or can state the maximum turnaround time he can tolerate at any price (the completion time specified or CTS rule).[14] Sharpe points out that, in the former case, price would be known and turnaround time uncertain, and, in the latter case, maximum turnaround time would be known but price would be uncertain.[15] In fact, if the computer system is highly congested, there is no assurance that the maximum turn-around-time constraint in the CTS method would be met at any price. The major disadvantage of flexible pricing schemes appears to be the uncertainty resulting from them.

Flexible microsequencing rules respond dynamically to changes in various parameters of the queueing system. Jackson, for example, proposes a rule whereby a job's priority is related to the length of time that it has been waiting in line.[16] This is another way of defining the job value functions in terms of the concepts presented here and implies a constant or increasing loss in value with increases in turnaround time.

Internal/External Allocation and Internal Regulation

In Chapter 5, a marginal pricing rule, based on value differences, was derived to induce users to allocate their computing budgets effectively between internal and external computing facilities. In this chapter, it was suggested that pricing can achieve the dynamic regulation of demand for internal computing. The following paragraph considers the conditions under which a single pricing policy can achieve both goals.

[14]S. Smidt. "Flexible Pricing."

[15]W. F. Sharpe. *Economics of Computers,* p. 469.

[16]J. R. Jackson. "Queues with Dynamic Priority Discipline." *Management Science,* 8:18–34, October 1961.

If the ET_t schedules for internal and external facilities are fairly constant throughout the period, and if no other controls are in effect, then the marginal-value-difference pricing rule will be effective in its goal of distributing jobs between internal and external computer facilities. Furthermore, if the value of running a job externally is greater than the value of running it internally by a given margin for all times during the period for all external and internal priorities, then the marginal-value-difference pricing rule can be effective in allocating jobs between internal and external processing. On the other hand, when the margin between the internal and external ET_t schedules at different priorities is not consistently positive or negative, the derivation of a pricing rule to allocate demand between internal and external facilities becomes highly complex and may not be feasible.

SPECIFIC CASES OF VALUE HILLS

This section examines the way value hills with particular shapes respond to various types of control measures.

Case I: Value Insensitive to Submission Time

In this case, the value of a job is independent of the time of submission, T_s, throughout the given period but is a function of the expected turnaround time. This is shown in Figure 24. The relationship between the value of the job and the expected turnaround time is the same for all relevant values of T_s. The value function of job i may be any monotonically nonincreasing function, as established previously.

If no controls are in effect, a user will submit the job at the T_s for which the ET_t schedule (shown by the broken line, ABC, in Figure 24) is a minimum, since this is the point at which the value of the job has a maximum of 3.4. Since the ET_t schedule in Figure 24 has a unique minimum at B, the user maximizes the value of the job by submitting it at time T_s^*. With multiple equal minima, as might occur when the ET_t schedule is flat, the user is indifferent to the selection of a T_s among those yielding maximum value and will select a T_s at random from among the available minima.

This type of value hill is particularly sensitive to peak-load pricing rules, since it generally will respond significantly to differences in price over time. If the expected turnaround time is constant throughout the period, the job will be submitted during a period of minimum price.

In a system with many jobs having this type of value hill, the

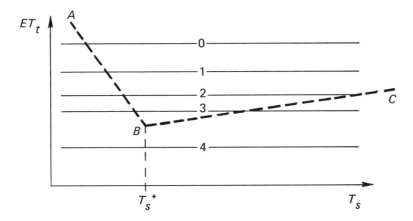

Figure 24   Value hill with value independent of the time of submission and dependent on the expected value of the turnaround time.

dynamic interaction between the value hills and the ET_t schedule will tend to be unstable when no specific controls are in effect. The pattern of job submissions is likely to fluctuate widely even with slight changes in the ET_t schedule. In order to stabilize the process, it is necessary to introduce controls, such as pricing and priority rules. This type of value hill is typically very responsive to such control measures. In summary, the type of job that is insensitive to T_s is responsive to the ET_t schedule emanating from the iterative feedback process and also is very conducive to direct controls.

In practice, many appointment systems exhibit this type of job value function since the user (e.g., a patient visiting a physician on a nonemergency basis) may be relatively indifferent to the time of the visit. This is particularly true for a periodic medical checkup that might be arranged months in advance. Once a patient arrives for service, the cost of waiting can be highly sensitive to the length of time awaiting service, particularly for a patient who is prepared for surgery which is then postponed. Such a situation not only causes anxiety for the patient but also extends the hospital stay, which is costly.

Analogous to the appointment scheme are train, bus, and airline schedules, since scheduled arrival or departure times are, in effect, appointments. If a train does not arrive on time, the traveller will be delayed in reaching his destination. This cost of lateness can cause both inconvenience and (perhaps) direct money costs. Tardiness in airline schedules may be exacerbated if connecting flights are missed, with a resulting cascading of lateness. The cost of waiting in an appointment situation is likely to increase much more rapidly over time than for random arrivals, since users would not expect to be delayed when an appointment (or schedule) has been prearranged and therefore will incur higher delay costs due to the unexpected variance in waiting time.

Case II: Value Positive at a Single Submission Time

At the other extreme is the job for which the value function does not exist except at one specific value of T_s. In Figure 25, the dots represent value levels and are equivalent to the contour notation of the value hill. The value function of job i only exists at submission time X; if the job is submitted at any other time, its value is zero. Consequently, the user will submit the job at time X or not at all, since there is no reason to submit it at any other time.

In this case, any control measure only influences the decision as to whether or not the job is submitted; it cannot change the submission time. Furthermore, if all the jobs in a system are of this type, the ET_t schedule and any direct controls will affect only the total number of jobs submitted, since the fundamental arrival time of a job is unalterable. A system containing a majority of this type of job will tend to be stable because the pattern of job submissions will tend to be unvarying. An oscillatory situation may exist, however, since a certain group of

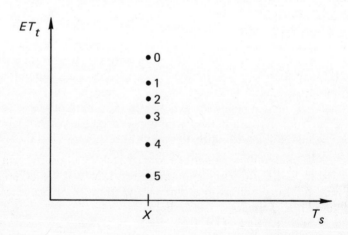

Figure 25   Value hill for a job for which the value function exists at a single T_s.

jobs may produce an ET_t schedule that induces a different grouping to be submitted. This, in turn, causes an ET_t schedule that brings about the first grouping, and so on. A system comprising Case II jobs generally is more stable than one consisting of Case I jobs, which is inherently unstable. Furthermore, a Case II system usually will converge much more rapidly to some equilibrium. The Case II type job may be considered as a restraining mechanism on the system, analogous to a damper in dynamic mechanical systems.

In general, the more sensitive the jobs in a system are to the time of submission, the more stable the system will be and the more rapidly it will converge to some equilibrium.

Although the Case II scenario is somewhat rare, it may be closely compared to the situation in which a store requests customer credit approval by telephone from a terminal operator at a central location. The operator has access to an on-line data base containing credit information and either authorizes or disapproves the transaction. Often, the customer is available only momentarily; if the central authorization agency cannot be contacted immediately, he or she may decide not to make the purchase or to return at another time when access to credit authorization is more readily available. In this case, the feasible submission time is of short duration.

Once contact with the authorizing agency has been made, the customer is likely to wait for the transaction to be completed; however, the store will incur costs of delay in response time, such as telephone-line charges, the opportunity cost of the server being available to other customers, the customer's annoyance and frustration (with possible loss of future business), and so on. Consequently, the value hill does show a dependence on turnaround time.

This example is analogous, but not identical, to the situation created in the control model, since the users are not employed within the organization. It does illustrate how an unusual value hill, as in Figure 25, might arise.

Case III: Jobs with Deadlines

A job that has a deadline has no value if it does not complete processing by a specific completion time, regardless of the submission time; that is, the sum of the submission time and the expected turnaround time (which is the completion time) cannot exceed the deadline time.[17] An example of a drop to zero value at the deadline

---

[17]The use of the expected value of the turnaround-time distribution is somewhat arbitrary, since it implies that (assuming a unimodal symmetric distribution of T_t) the user

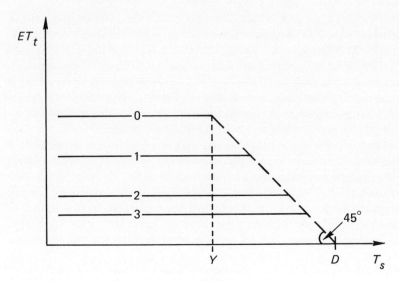

Figure 26   Value hill for job with deadline at *D*.

time is characterized by the diagonal boundary to the value hill of Figure 26, where D is the deadline time. The general shape of the value hill will depend on its sensitivity to the time of submission and turnaround time. The deadline results in a zero-value contour with a minus-one gradient, as shown in Figure 26.

The sensitivity of this type of job to direct controls and changes in the ET_t schedule depends in some measure on the shape of the contours behind the deadline boundary. In Figure 26, the job behaves like a Case I job up to a submission time of Y, in that its value is dependent on ET_t only (and insensitive to T_s) up to the deadline. Such a job responds significantly to changes in the ET_t schedule and to control measures prior to time Y. For submission times between Y and D, the response is restricted by the deadline boundary, and the job behaves more like a Case II job, with less sensitivity to the ET_t schedule.

This value hill can be illustrated as a variation of the appointment scheme described in Case I. For example, an individual might be relatively indifferent as to which train he catches over a range of time; however, as the deadline at the end of the trip approaches (e.g., getting to work or to an important meeting on time), the individual becomes

---

will be satisfied if the deadline is met 50 percent of the time. In general, some upper confidence limit may be used.

very sensitive to whether the latest train that, according to the schedule, would get him to his destination on time, departs on time. It is assumed that the journey is of fixed duration; that is, if the train departs late, it arrives at least as late, unless it makes up time during the journey. This is analogous to a single-programmed computer, where a job, once initiated, takes over the machine. Its processing time is independent of other jobs requiring service. In a multiprogramming environment, the computer operator often has the flexibility to vary the priorities of jobs in the system and, under emergency conditions, can flush all other jobs from active processing and devote all available resources to a particular job. The latter situation, in which the microsequencing features can be manipulated, makes for a system responsive to value hills of the form described in the next section.

Figure 27 shows a somewhat different deadline value hill with parallel iso-value lines, all at 45 degrees to the horizontal axis; that is, they have a minus-one gradient. This value hill is similar to the righthand half of the generalized deadline example shown in Figure 20(c). Usually, only the part shown in Figure 27 is of interest for microsequencing purposes, whereas the entire value hill should be included for macrosequencing. If the job is submitted at X_1 or X_2, with turnaround times Y_1 and Y_2, respectively, the value is 4 units in either case and the completion times are the same: $(X_1 + Y_1) = (X_2 + Y_2)$. Sharpe implies this form of value hill by relating value to completion time.[18]

Critical deadlines, which are a way of life for most organizations, occur due to fixed time requirements, such as tax-filing dates, contractual dates (employees' paydays), or the date and time by which bids must be submitted in order to be considered. The cost of missing deadlines varies with the particular case. For example, if a tax-filing date is missed, the Internal Revenue Service will impose a fine; if a payday is missed, employees will become irate; and if a bid is submitted late, millions of dollars of potential business might be lost. Similarly, if a student does not complete course requirements on time, he might not receive credit for the course until the following semester, which might delay his graduation.

The costs of missing deadlines range from minor to catastrophic. This difference is represented in the value hill by the maximum value and the rate of decline in value. In some cases, missing a deadline will cause a reduction in value, although some value for the job will be retained at a lower level. This would be the case when a penalty or fine

[18]W. F. Sharpe. *Economics of Computers,* p. 470.

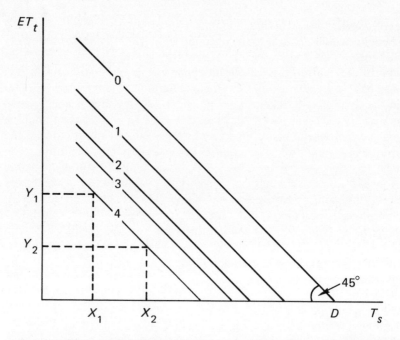

Source: C. W. Axelrod. "Effective Use of Computer Resources," p. 324. Reprinted by permission of Pergamon Press.

Figure 27   Value hill for job with deadline where value is the same for the same completion time.

is incurred if the deadline is missed, such as the loss of a discount that is given if a bill is paid within 30 days, but where it is necessary to process the payment in any event. A further value loss would occur subsequently if the payee brought suit for nonpayment. Once a bid deadline is missed due to delays in computer processing, there is no longer any benefit in running the job. In this situation, the value hill would drop to zero at the deadline from a value representing the profit and other returns to be gained from submitting the bid (e.g., goodwill and a reputation for timeliness), adjusted for the probability of having won the bid and for the possibility of not being considered for future lucrative bids.

The General Case

The value of a job has been considered as being a function of the time of submission, T_s, and the expected turnaround time, ET_t; that is, the value of job i may be expressed as $v_i(T_s, ET_t)$. The effectiveness of direct controls and the ET_t schedule was shown to be related to the derivative (or slope) of the value hill with respect to the submission time, for a given expected turnaround time. This is expressed algebraically as:

$$\frac{\partial v_i}{\partial T_s}\bigg|_{ET_t}$$

which reads as "the partial derivative of v_i with respect to T_s, ET_t held constant." When the derivative tends to zero, the value hill becomes the series of horizontal parallel lines of Case I. When the derivative tends to infinity, the value hill approaches that of Case II.

The sensitivity of a job to submission time consequently can be expressed in terms of the above derivative, if it exists. Since the responsiveness of a job to controls and the ET_t schedule is directly related to the sensitivity of the job to T_s, an indication as to how sensitive a job is to control measures and changes in the system can be obtained by examining the value of the derivative at various expected turnaround times.

THE OPTIMIZATION OF THE GENERAL SYSTEM

The response of the user to the expected turnaround-time schedule and control measures such as peak-load pricing has been analyzed. The user was assumed to evaluate the effect of the system parameters and controls on the value hills of a job and to submit the job at the time, price, priority, and so on, that maximized the value of that job. It cannot be ensured that, by maximizing his own utility, a user will maximize the utility of the overall system, however this is defined. In fact, the individual user's maximization behavior typically will lead to suboptimization of the whole system. The role of the controls instigated by central control is to induce individual users to maximize the utility of the system while maximizing their own utilities, subject to the imposed constraints.

In a system that is heavily utilized, a job that enters the system at a specific time usually will impose a loss in value on all other jobs that are delayed because of extended waiting times.

Value Loss as a Function of Submission Time

If the parameters of the system (such as the arrival pattern and service rate) are known, the waiting times and processing times may be estimated over a range of submission times for each job, assuming that an individual job does not significantly affect the characteristics of the queueing system. Because generally the queue length will vary over time, the ET_t schedule confronting a job also will vary throughout the given period, as shown in Figure 28(a), so that the value of running the job will tend to vary with time, even if the job value function is relatively insensitive to submission time. Figure 28(b) shows the ET_t schedule of Figure 28(a) as a broken line intersecting the value hill for job i. The points at which the ET_t schedule cuts the value hill provide the values of job i were it submitted at the various times along the horizontal axis. By projecting the value levels along the ET_t schedule in Figure 28(b) onto the T_s axis, the curve in Figure 28(c) is obtained. This shows the job value as a function of T_s. Furthermore, the variation in queue length implies that a job will delay a different group of jobs, depending on when it is submitted, which generally will lead to value loss (due to the job) varying with the time of submission of the job. This is the *total value loss function* illustrated in Figure 28(d).

The *net gain function* of job i, shown in Figure 28(e), is the difference between the value of job i and the loss in value due to job i, expressed as a function of submission time.

The Best Submission Time

If there are no pricing or budget controls, the user would respond to the ET_t schedule and value hill by submitting job i at time X, which, as indicated in Figure 28(c), yields the maximum value, V_X, to the user. It can be shown, however, from the total value loss function of Figure 28(d), that job i imposes a total loss of L_X on the system when submitted at time X, so that the net gain to the system from job i is GT_X, which equals $V_X - L_X$, as shown in Figure 28(e). Although the maximum net gain accruing to the system, G_Y, occurs in this case when job i is submitted at time Y, the user would not autonomously submit job i at Y, because it would cause a drop in value from his maximum of V_X to V_Y [see Figure 28(c)]. If it is concluded that, taking all other jobs into consideration, it is desirable to submit job i at Y, then central control must institute either a pricing rule or a specific schedule that will induce the user to submit the job at Y, without the system incurring any loss in total value.

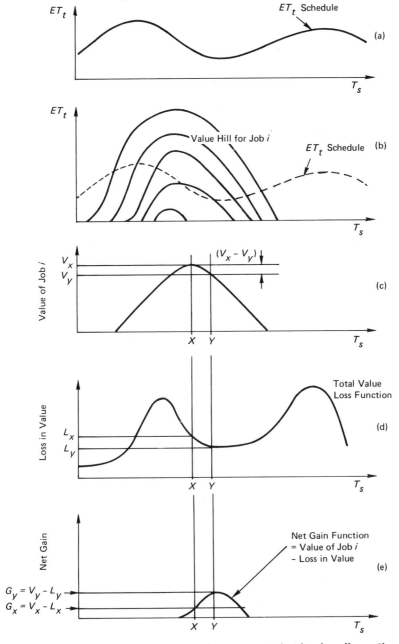

Figure 28 The sequence of procedures to attain the locally optimal time of submission for a job.

Dolan develops a "pricing mechanism based on the expected marginal delay cost which a user's service imposes on other users of the service facility."[19] He proves that setting the price equal to the marginal cost of delay imposed on other users allows central control to allocate resources optimally and to minimize total delay costs.

Examples of Value Loss Due to Delay

It is assumed that job i has processing time p_i, all jobs are of the same type, the computer is in the single-processing mode, and the queue discipline is first-come-first-served (FCFS). If the probability distributions of the arrival and service times and the queue discipline are known, the distribution of the waiting time may be obtained. The mean arrival rate is independent of time and is denoted by $\bar{r}_a$. The expected value of the waiting time distribution is $\bar{w}$.

Jobs that arrive for service after job i has entered the system, but before job i has completed service, are delayed to some extent by the processing of job i. Queue disciplines other than FCFS will result in different delay patterns. The time interval during which jobs can be delayed by job i is the sum of the expected waiting time and the processing time of job i, $(\bar{w} + p_i)$, so that the expected number of jobs that will be affected by the presence of job i is $\bar{r}_a(\bar{w} + p_i)$, since jobs are processed FCFS. Jobs arriving during $\bar{w}$ will each be delayed p_i time units by job i, whereas those jobs arriving while job i is being processed will be delayed for a period of time between zero and p_i time units—an average of $p_i/2$ units. The total delay caused to all other jobs in the system by job i is:

$$d^{(i)} = p_i \bar{r}_a \bar{w} + \frac{p_i^2 \bar{r}_a}{2}.$$

Because the value of a job is a monotonically nonincreasing function of the expected turnaround time, the introduction of job i into the system and the resulting delay will lead to a loss in the value of all jobs delayed by job i that have strictly decreasing value functions over the relevant time interval. In certain relatively simple cases, the calculation of the value loss is obtained fairly easily from the total delay and the value loss per job. For complex value hills and sequencing rules, however,

[19]R. J. Dolan. "Priority Pricing Models for Congested Systems." Working Paper Series No. 7710. Rochester, N.Y., Graduate School of Management, University of Rochester, 1977, p. iv. Mimeographed.

the evaluation process can be time consuming because full enumeration may be required. The following are examples of methods for obtaining the aggregate value loss due to delay for populations of jobs with value functions with particular shapes, such as the constant and variable gradient with respect to expected turnaround time.

1. *Constant Gradient Value Functions:*

   a. *All Jobs with the Same Gradient*

   If the value functions of all jobs delayed by job i have the same constant slope with respect to expected turnaround time over the relevant expected turnaround-time range, then each time unit of delay costs the same value loss. Consequently, the total loss in value is given by the product of $d^{(i)}$ (which is the sum of the delays for all jobs suffering delay due to job i) and the constant rate of value loss.

   b. *Jobs Having Constant, but Different, Gradients*

   If the rate of change in value with respect to expected turnaround time is constant over time for all jobs delayed by job i, but the constant value is different for different jobs, it is necessary to calculate the value loss for each job (i.e., the delay experienced by the job, multiplied by the constant rate of change in value), and add together the individual jobs' value losses to obtain the total value loss.

2. *Variable Gradient Value Functions:* When the gradient of the value function is not constant, it is not possible to calculate the value loss in so straightforward a manner, since the magnitude of the gradient varies with the expected turnaround time. The loss in value due to the delay must be obtained for each job from its value function.

For example, consider job k, which would have received service at time s_k if job i were omitted, and which requires p_k units of processing time. If $v_j(t)$ is the value of job j when it completes service at time t, job k would have a value of $v_k(s_k + p_k)$ if job i does not precede it, and a value of $v_k(s_k + p_k + p_i)$ in the case where job i does precede it, assuming job k arrives while job i is waiting to enter service. The value loss[20] experienced by job k due to its being delayed by job i is

$$v_k(s_k + p_k + p_i) - v_k(s_k + p_k).$$

---

[20]This value loss is nonnegative, since the value function is nonincreasing with respect to ET_t.

The total value loss due to job i is obtained by aggregating the individual losses of jobs, substituting fractions of p_i for p_i when jobs arrive during the processing of job i. This procedure holds for all value functions, whether or not the gradient of the value function is constant with respect to expected turnaround time. The actual value loss is dependent on the order in which jobs are submitted, the processing time and type of each job, and the microsequencing rule in operation.

Problem of Measuring Value Loss

In a system which has a high rate of throughput, an individual job may cause a negligible delay on any succeeding job. Under typical conditions, it may not be possible to determine individual job value losses accurately because the losses per job may be negligible; however, when accumulated over large numbers of jobs, even very small value losses become significant. It should be adequate in most practical instances to use the technique described previously in 1.a., using some estimated average rate of value loss, as an approximation. This is the easiest and cheapest method, yet generally it will produce valuable results, sufficient for most decision making.

SUMMARY

The concept of the multivariate job value function, dependent both upon various system characteristics (such as ET_t) and clock time, was introduced. The effects of peak-load pricing and priority rules on the value function were examined. In the latter section, the value loss due to delay was considered in the context of using value function analysis for scheduling.

7

MICROSEQUENCING: CONTROL OF THE ORDER OF PROCESSING

THE FUNCTION OF MICROSEQUENCING IN THE MODEL

A microsequencing rule is one that regulates the order in which jobs that have been entered into the system are processed. In the specification of the value function model, little attention has been given to the effects of particular microsequencing rules; however, an integral part of the model is turnaround-time distribution, which depends significantly on the rules that determine the sequence in which jobs are serviced once they have entered the system. Therefore, in this chapter, specific microsequencing rules will be examined in the context of the value function model.

The Objectives of Microsequencing

A microsequencing rule should:

1. Sequence jobs so as to maximize the total value of jobs processed in a given period (i.e., system effectiveness).
2. Encourage users to design their jobs so as to make efficient use of the computer facilities (i.e., discourage users from using the system inefficiently).

Factors Determining the Sequencing of Jobs

Many microsequencing rules have been proposed in the literature on operations research. These rules, some of which will be re-

119

viewed in the following section, may be categorized as: time-dependent rules, rules dependent on job parameters, and value-oriented rules. The rules that are expressed in terms of time or job characteristics, rather than value, generally are based on implicit assumptions regarding the form of the value functions. The implied value functions of a number of microsequencing rules will be examined.

TIME-DEPENDENT SEQUENCING RULES

Time-dependent sequencing rules are based on specific time parameters of the *system,* such as the arrival times of jobs and the time spent awaiting service. They are not related to specific characteristics of either the jobs or the service station. Three time-dependent rules will be described: first-come-first-served (FCFS), last-in-first-out (LIFO), and random service.

First-Come-First-Served Discipline

With the FCFS rule, jobs are processed in the sequence in which they arrive for service in a single-queue system. If two or more jobs arrive for service simultaneously, a different rule must be invoked to break the tie.[1] The FCFS rule also may be interpreted as one in which jobs are processed in the order of longest waiting time in the queue.

PROPERTIES OF THE FCFS RULE

Jobs having the longest waiting time have the highest priority, so that the maximum waiting time tends to be lower than with other rules. Operationally, the FCFS discipline is relatively easy to administer. The computer center must know only the arrival times of jobs and must have a search procedure to select from the queue the job with the earliest arrival time (i.e., the longest waiting time).

CONDITIONS FOR OPTIMALITY OF THE FCFS RULE

Jackson indicates that FCFS schedules will be optimal if the delay-cost functions of waiting times are symmetric functions satisfying a mild convexity condition—"symmetry-convex."[2] Intuitively, if

---

[1] Jobs may begin service simultaneously in a multiserver system.
[2] J. R. Jackson. "First-come-first-served Scheduling Is Often Optimal. Part I: Symmetry-Convexity." Western Management Science Institute Working Paper No. 125. Los Angeles, University of California, 1967.

the rate of change of delay cost increases with the length of time spent waiting in line, users will incur losses in value at an increased rate with respect to waiting time. Consequently, there is an incentive to reduce excessive waiting time for any job, which is the prime feature of the FCFS rule. The type of value function (expressed as a function of expected turnaround time) that would indicate use of the FCFS rule is shown in Figure 29.

Last-In-First-Out Discipline

With the LIFO scheduling rule, jobs are processed in the reverse sequence to that in which they arrived for service; that is, when the server becomes available, the job that arrived most recently (the job that has been waiting in line for the shortest time) is the one that enters service. As with the FCFS rule, when jobs arrive simultaneously, some other rule must be used to break the tie.

PROPERTIES OF THE LIFO RULE

The LIFO rule serves to increase the maximum queueing time and to decrease the minimum queueing time. Operationally, this rule is very similar to the FCFS rule in that the computer center needs to

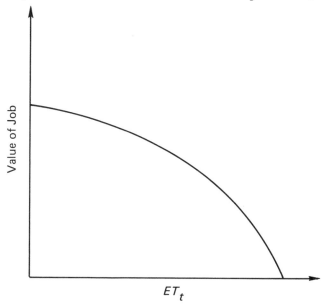

Figure 29 Value function with the rate of value loss an increasing function of expected turnaround time.

know only the arrival times of jobs in order to sequence them in LIFO order.

CONDITIONS FOR OPTIMALITY OF THE LIFO RULE

Clearly, this rule favors jobs that have high values at short turnaround times and low values for moderate and long turnaround times. LIFO is most suitable for cases in which the value initially falls off rapidly with respect to waiting time and steadily maintains a relatively low value at longer waiting times, as shown in Figure 30.

Random Microsequencing

With random microsequencing, jobs are selected for processing at random from the jobs awaiting service when a server becomes available. The time at which a job arrives is irrelevant to when it enters service.

PROPERTIES OF THE RANDOM MICROSEQUENCING RULE

Compared to the FCFS and LIFO rules, the random rule is operationally simpler, because it does not require that the computer center know the arrival time of a job, merely that the job is available for

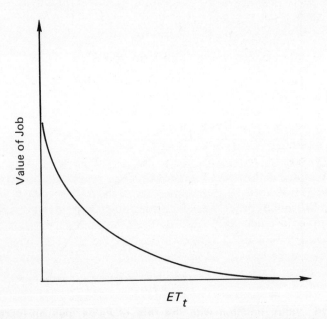

Figure 30 Value function with the rate of value loss a decreasing function of expected turnaround time.

service. No job is given priority on any basis. The probability that a job may be selected in a given time interval may be obtained from arrival and service patterns and from characteristics of the system.

CONDITIONS FOR OPTIMALITY OF THE RANDOM MICROSEQUENCING RULE

The random microsequencing rule implicity assumes that the rates of value loss are independent of the time at which jobs begin service, which is valid if the value functions of all jobs are nonincreasing linear functions of waiting time with the same gradient and if they exist (i.e., are positive) throughout the entire period. In this case, the random service rule will result in the same total net value as the LIFO and FCFS rules, since the sequence in which jobs are run will not affect the value. The implementation of the LIFO and FCFS rules tends to be more costly than the random service rule, so the latter will yield the highest total net value when the value functions are linear in waiting time and have the same gradient.

RULES DEPENDENT ON JOB PARAMETERS

Under these rules, jobs are sequenced according to one or more of their physical attributes, such as job size, job type, or a combination of job size and type.

Microsequencing Based on Job Size

Two specific rules will be considered here: the shortest-job-first (SJF) and the longest-job-first (LJF).

SHORTEST-JOB-FIRST RULE

Under the shortest-job-first (SJF) or shortest-processing-time (SPT) rule, of those jobs in the queue, the job with the shortest processing time is the first to be run when the service station becomes available. If two jobs are of the same size, a rule that is related to some other factor should be used to determine sequence. If many jobs in a queue are of the same size, then another rule, such as FCFS, may have to be used in conjunction with or instead of the SJF rule. When many jobs of the same size make up the queue, the job-size-oriented rule loses its effectiveness, and the secondary rule that is used to break ties will dominate.

Properties of the SJF Rule   The SJF rule tends to reduce the mean waiting time of jobs, but it also increases the variance of the waiting time. Only job sizes need to be known to perform the primary scheduling (as opposed to tie-breaking secondary rules). Because in practice the actual processing time may not be known prior to service, an estimate may have to be used.

Conditions for Optimality of the SJF Rule   If preemption is not permitted (i.e., if a job cannot be interrupted and rescheduled once it begins processing), the sjf rule reduces the average job's turnaround time, thus reducing the total waiting time for all jobs.[3] This minimization is achieved at the expense of increasing the variance of job waiting times. The rule penalizes a lengthy job that may be subjected to an excessively long wait if many short jobs are in the queue or arrive while it is waiting. This trade-off between reduction of mean waiting time and increase in variance implies that users generally prefer to wait less time at the expense of occasionally having an excessive waiting time. The computer center operating under the sjf rule implicitly assumes that shorter jobs have a more rapid initial fall-off in value with respect to expected turnaround time than longer jobs, so that the smallest value loss is achieved by processing the short jobs as soon after their arrival as possible.

LONGEST-JOB-FIRST RULE

Under the longest-job-first (ljf) rule, also called the longest-processing-time (lpt) rule, of those jobs in the queue, the job with the longest processing time is the first to be run. In the case of ties, some other rule should be used.

Properties of the LJF Rule   The ljf rule maximizes the total waiting time of jobs, because the mean waiting time also is maximized. Intuitively, the variance of the waiting time distribution will be less than under the sjf and fcfs rules. Operationally, the ljf and sjf rules are similar.

Conditions for Optimality of the LJF Rule   The ljf rule is used in circumstances where the values of the longer jobs exhibit a more rapid falloff, with increases in mean waiting time relative to short jobs. Implicitly, in the use of the ljf rule, the computer center assumes that the values of jobs are relatively insensitive to the mean waiting time but that the values do decrease significantly as the variance of the waiting time distribution increases.

[3]W. F. Sharpe. *The Economics of Computers*. New York, Columbia University Press, 1969, p. 480.

RANDOM SERVICE

Such rules as FCFS and LIFO, which are based on the arrival time of jobs, do not take into account the size of the jobs. Consequently, the microsequencing rules can be considered to be random with respect to job size, assuming that there is no correlation between arrival time and job size.

Microsequencing Based on Job Type

It has been presumed that processing times do not depend on the order in which jobs are processed. In a single-programming situation, the setup time for a job may depend on the type of job that preceded it. Typically, economies of setup time may be achieved if jobs of the same type are grouped together. In a multiprogramming system, different type jobs may be run in specific combinations—based on their compatibility—that are more efficient than if they are run in a sequence based on time of arrival or job length. Such an approach may include balancing the mix of compute bound jobs and input-output bound jobs resident in the machine at one time.

By sequencing the jobs, a scheduler can minimize the total waiting time by reducing total setup time in single-programming cases and increasing machine utilization for multiprogramming. The minimization of waiting time, however, may not ensure value loss minimization. When the rule specifies that jobs of the same type should be run together, they may be delayed excessively, with a resultant high loss of value, if the system is flooded with jobs of another type already being processed. To counter this effect, a rule such as the alternating priority discipline is used. With this system, a limited number of jobs of one type (or priority) are processed, after which the service is relinquished to another type.[4]

Rules Based on Job Size, Type, and Arrival Time

Just as time-dependent and job-size-dependent rules may be used in primary-secondary combinations to break ties, a combination of rules that depend on the type of job and rules that depend on arrival time and job size may be desirable.[5]

[4]For example, see L. W. Miller, "Alternating Priorities in Multi-Class Queues," Doctoral Dissertation, Ithaca, N.Y., Cornell University, 1964.

[5]Complex microsequencing rules, comprised of a combination of different rules, are quite common in actual computer centers (especially a combination such as FCFS and priority classes).

Operationally, there is an increase in complexity and information requirements when job types are a determining sequencing factor. Classification of jobs into a few simple categories, such as compute bound and input-output bound may be sufficient; however, the number of job parameters may be large, in which case the number of scheduling operations will increase combinatorially.[6] Clearly, an economic trade-off between efficient machine utilization and scheduling costs must be achieved.

VALUE-ORIENTED RULES

The aforementioned rules were not explicitly determined by the value functions of jobs, although they could be described as having some implicit underlying value-functional form. The rules in this section are derived explicitly from the value functions of jobs. The following types of value-oriented rules shall be considered: priorities based on job value, priorities based on user status, price-based rules, and sequencing with preemption.

Priorities Based on Job Value

The net value of a job may depend on tangible parameters, such as the mean and variance of the turnaround-time distribution and the submission time, and it may include more obscure factors, such as inconvenience and aggravation.[7] Much of the work in this area is concerned with value functions of the actual or expected waiting time. The possible influence of uncertainty has been alluded to, but there is no explicit analysis involving uncertainty.

PROPERTIES OF VALUE-BASED RULES

Generally, nonpreemptive rules examine the value functions of jobs in the queue and select a sequence that maximizes the total

[6]See N. Nielsen, "Flexible Pricing: An Approach to the Allocation of Computer Resources," in: *Proceedings of 1968 AFIPS Fall Joint Computer Conference, San Francisco*, Montvale, N.J., AFIPS Press, 1968, pp. 521–531.

[7]Lynch describes how the Case Institute of Technology computer center intended to replace the SJF rule with one based on a nonlinear function of the estimated running time and time spent waiting in the queue to "minimize customer aggravation." See W. C. Lynch, "Description of a High Capacity Fast Turnaround University Computer Center," in: *Proceedings of 22nd National Conference*, edited by the Association for Computing Machinery, Washington, D.C., Thompson Book Company, 1967, pp. 273–288, ACM Publication P-67.

value of jobs processed.[8] It is more usual to find, in the operations research literature, references to the cost of waiting rather than the reduction in value due to waiting. Value-based rules fall into two categories, algorithmic rules and heuristic search rules, depending on the complexity of the value functions.

Algorithmic Rules   In practice, algorithmic rules apply in cases of simple forms of the value function and are usually constant or linear with respect to waiting time, as in Dolan's work.[9] Greenberger considers a general rule:[10] integration of the rate of change of waiting cost from an initial time to the time of completion, for all possible job sequences, and selection of that sequence which provides the minimum cost. With nonlinear cost/rate curves, the determination of the optimal sequence tends to be cumbersome, although some degree of simplification is possible with exponentially discounted cost rates. When the cost rates are constant or linear, a simple rule may be used.

If all jobs in a system have the same constant cost/rate curves (i.e., the net value functions are linear nonincreasing functions of turnaround time, with the slope of all curves being equal), then the minimization of cost accrual, or value loss, is equivalent to minimizing average expected turnaround. Of the nonpreemptive microsequencing rules discussed so far, the SJF rule minimizes the average waiting time and, therefore, would be optimal in this case.

If all jobs have constant, but possibly different, cost/rate curves, then the c/t rule is optimal, assuming a single-server situation. This rule states that, if c_i is the constant cost rate of job i in the queue and t_i is its expected processing time, then the job for which the c_i/t_i ratio is highest should be served next.[11] When all the c_i are equal, the c/t rule reduces to the SJF rule. In value function terms, the c/t ratio becomes the ratio of the absolute value of the derivative of the linear value function divided by the expected processing time for the job.

A differentiation must be made between *lateness*, which is defined as

---

[8]W. F. Sharpe. *Economics of Computers*, pp. 476–477. Sharpe considers an example in which the optimality of the sequence of jobs already in the system depends on the characteristics of jobs that have not yet arrived.

[9]R. J. Dolan. "Priority Pricing Models for Congested Systems." Working Paper Series No. 7710. Rochester, N.Y., Graduate School of Management, University of Rochester, 1977. Mimeographed.

[10]M. Greenberger. "The Priority Problem and Computer Time Sharing." *Management Science, 12*:888–906, July 1966.

[11]For a proof of the c/t rules, see R. McNaughton, "Scheduling with Deadlines and Loss Functions," *Management Science, 6*:1–12, October 1959.

the difference between a job's completion time and its due time (this difference may be positive or negative), and *tardiness,* which is defined as "rectified lateness"; that is, it includes positive lateness only.[12] If value loss is directly proportional to the difference between completion and due time, lateness is exemplified by a linear value function and tardiness by a piecewise linear function, with zero gradient up to the due time and a constant negative gradient thereafter. The lateness case is readily handled by the c/t rule, whereas the tardiness example does not generally lend itself to so simple an approach. The tardiness case may, of course, be resolved using the generalized Greenberger approach. It has been shown, however, that algorithmic techniques may be used to minimize certain functions of job tardiness.[13]

Heuristic Search Methods To obtain efficient schedules for value functions of other than the most simple form, it is a practical necessity to use heuristics to reduce the number of operations involved in exhaustive searches.

Priorities Based on User Status

In systems that handle large numbers of jobs, it sometimes is convenient to group job value functions into categories that are determined by the type of user submitting the job or the type of project of which the job is a part. Although such classification may not be as precise as individual job valuation, the cost savings of implementation may substantially outweigh the probable value losses resulting from misclassified jobs. In other systems, the individual user may divide his workload into various priority classes; however, users may abuse a flexible system by running unimportant jobs at higher priorities than necessary, simply because the higher level of service is available. An intermediate system might award individual users specific priority classifications with limitations on usage at specific priorities.

Typically, in a university, faculty have higher user status for computer resources than graduate students, and graduates have higher status than undergraduates. Budgets and priorities generally are assigned according to this hierarchy. This requires relatively simple budgetary and priority rules. A problem, however, is that not *all* faculty use of the computer is more important to the institution than *all*

---

[12]See H. Emmons, "One-Machine Sequencing to Minimize Certain Functions of Job Tardiness," *Operations Research, 17*:701–715, July–August 1969.
[13]*Ibid.*

graduate and undergraduate use—although for the most part it may be so. Such a situation points out a shortcoming of this simplified form of priority assignment—it does not consider the value of the jobs, which might be highly variable, particularly over time.

In business, computer jobs are likely to be for production, maintenance, or research and development purposes. These categories can be considered as belonging to a job value breakdown, with production and development jobs exhibiting different value function forms. Generally, the development, production, and maintenance functions reside in separate departments, so that computer jobs may indeed be classified by department and, hence, status of the user. Occasionally, an individual might perform more than one such function (e.g., development and maintenance), in which case the classification procedure should consider this distinction. In any event, in most business environments, production jobs are given the highest priority, with maintenance taking precedence during emergencies. Usually, regular maintenance is secondary to production, and research and development has the lowest priority. Sometimes development may take precedence over batch production work that can be run at night, because the development user, who is acutely aware of the response time of the computer system (especially on time-sharing), may be more vocal than the production user, who may accept a long turnaround time for a particular job and probably is not monitoring its progress. If the machine were to go down for an extended period, thereby threatening the completion of the batch production job by its deadline, true user status would be acknowledged, and the production work would take precedence. The computer center's responsiveness to the complaining development user is highly dependent on the urgency expressed by the higher status production users.

Price-Based Sequencing Rules

A user may be allotted a budget and the freedom to select any of a number of priority levels, the higher priorities being available at higher prices. The user's choice of priority will be based on the priority/price relationship, his funds, his particular service needs, and the state of congestion in the system. Such rules do not depend on the predetermination of job values or user priorities by the computer center, since users presumably evaluate specific jobs just prior to submission. To achieve the level of control of the other rules, however, the budget allocation must be made accurately in order to attain a funds distribution that equalizes the marginal utility of budgets for all users.

This would appear to confound the support of such rules as being more efficient and responsive to the dynamics of the system.

In practice, users may be allocated funds and an upper priority level and may be free to select the priority deemed adequate to provide the desired level of service. The priority levels and their prices are known at the start of the period. In other cases, price and priority are determined dynamically in response to the state of the system. As discussed in Chapter 6, Smidt suggests two such rules: completion time specified (CTS) and maximum rate specified (MRS).[14] Under the CTS rule, users agree to pay the "going rate" required to realize a turnaround time that is within a specified limit. With MRS scheduling, the user provides the service center with a maximum price that he will pay and accepts whatever turnaround time this entails. Both rules generate user uncertainty: the CTS rule with respect to the price to be paid and the MRS with regard to the turnaround time. Furthermore, if the system is overloaded, the specific CTS turnaround-time limit may not be feasible at any price.

Microsequencing with Preemption

It has been assumed that once a job begins service, its processing is not interrupted until it has completed service. If the processing is interrupted to allow processing of another job that is awaiting service, the rule is termed preemptive. Subsequent to preemption, a job may be discarded completely, may be resumed where processing ended, or may be restarted, depending on both the rule in effect and the ability of the system to handle jobs in complex ways.

The Preemptive SJF Rule

If a job being processed is preempted by a new job that has a shorter processing time than the remaining processing time of the job being served but its processing is resumed at the point at which it was interrupted, the mean waiting time is less than that of the straightforward SJF rule (although the variance is greater), assuming a single server and instantaneous job interchange (i.e., when one job is removed from processing and another job is substituted, it is assumed that such an interchange, or swap, takes place instantaneously).[15]

[14]S. Smidt. "Flexible Pricing for Computer Services." *Management Science, 14*:B581–B600, June 1968.
[15]E. G. Coffman, Jr. and L. Kleinrock. "Computer Scheduling Methods and Their Countermeasures." In: *Proceedings of 1968 AFIPS Spring Joint Computer Conference, Atlantic City.* Montvale, N.J., AFIPS Press, 1968, p. 13.

Round-Robin (RR) Scheduling[16]

This type of rule typically involves the concept of processing quanta that are selected to optimize the operation of the system. Jobs initially are sequenced according to some other rule (such as FCFS), and then are processed for the length of the quantum, at which point the job is preempted and put at the end of the queue. When the job again reaches the service station, it is resumed. The job leaves the system when it has received sufficient quanta to fulfill its service requirements. The interval between successive service periods for a particular job depends on the number of jobs in line and the size of the quanta. If the quanta are small, the jobs receive frequent short intervals of service; however, the smaller the quanta, the greater the number of swaps and the higher the cost. Small quanta have the advantage of giving short jobs (one or two quanta in length) rapid turnaround times. Quanta that are long with respect to job size tend to reduce the RR effect, and the secondary scheduling rule will take a dominant role. A major advantage of this type of rule, compared to those that are based on job size, is that it is not necessary for the computer center to know the length of jobs in advance.

The Derivation of a Generalized Value-Based Rule

The microsequencing rules that have been examined so far either do not relate directly to the value functions of jobs or only consider simple value relationships. The rules that have been developed on the basis of job parameters or system parameters do bear upon the value of jobs. Deduction of the form of the value functions that might be inferred for the effective application of the nonvalue-oriented microsequencing rules also has been attempted. In this section, the opposite approach, namely, development of rules that increase the net value of running the jobs, given some collection of job value functions, will be presented.

In effect, the general approach is similar to that suggested by Greenberger,[17] although his analysis was in terms of cost-rate functions and this study considers the net value function. The difference between the two types of functions is that the value function at any T is equivalent to the value at time T_o minus the integral from T_o to T of the cost/rate function, that is, for job i,

$$v_i(T) = v_i(T_o) - \int_{T_o}^{T} c_i(t)dt.$$

[16]*Ibid.*, p. 14.
[17]M. Greenberger. "Priority Problem."

THE LINEAR AND TARDINESS CASES

The linear net value case (or the constant cost/rate case) has already been solved with the c/t rule. The tardiness case (i.e., linear total cost following a due time) has been examined by Emmons,[18] who also developed an extension to his algorithm for a loss function that is convex and increasing.[19]

THE OBJECTIVE OF THE GENERAL RULE

It was stated previously that microsequencing rules have the dual role of maximizing long-term total net value and inducing users to submit their most efficient jobs. The latter objective involves encouraging users to lessen the demand on the system per job: This can be accomplished by charging a shadow price equivalent to the value loss of marginal increases in job lengths.

THE VALUE FUNCTION FOR A GIVEN SUBMISSION TIME

If the value hill is a function of the expected turnaround time and the time of submission of the job only, then the value function to be considered for microsequencing is the value with respect to the expected turnaround time, *given* that the job was submitted at a specific time.

THE RATE OF LOSS IN NET VALUE

The major influencing features of the value function on the microsequencing rules are the first and second derivatives with respect to expected turnaround time, namely:

$$\left. \frac{\partial v_i}{\partial ET_t} \right|_{T_s} \quad \text{and} \quad \left. \frac{\partial^2 v_i}{\partial ET_t^2} \right|_{T_s}$$

If the gradient is constant and the second derivative is zero, it produces the linear cost case.

In general, a large negative gradient implies a rapid value loss and the need to run the job early relative to smaller value loss rates. If the second derivative with respect to ET_t is negative, implying that the urgency of the job increases over time, then the need to run the job early is enhanced over time. This latter type of function is shown in Figure 29.

---

[18]H. Emmons. "One-Machine Sequencing."
[19]*Ibid*.

A positive second derivative, as in Figure 30, suggests that the job should be run early in the sequence; however, if it is not run early, its urgency diminishes rapidly over time.

A small negative gradient represents a slow value loss, indicating that such a job should be superseded by jobs of larger negative slope. If the first derivative is small, but the second derivative is negative and large, the job will quickly reach a high degree of urgency (as in Figure 29), assuming that its initial net value is sufficiently high to prevent the value reaching zero before the urgency gets to be high.

SUMMARY

Whether they do so explicitly or not, all microsequencing rules subsume specific forms of the job value hills for their effectiveness. In this chapter, some of the underlying value implications of a number of microsequencing rules were examined and their conditions for optimality were determined.

PART III

8
SOME ILLUSTRATIVE EXAMPLES

Although the measurement of job value relative to turn-around time, submission time, and other factors is by no means simple, it is possible, through the use of well-designed questionnaires (such as those described in King and Bryant[1] and Mueller[2]), to obtain good approximations of users' estimates of the relative values of their various jobs. The absolute value ratings should be determined partly by a central authority using, perhaps, a priority system which is then integrated into the value function.

Even after such data have been collected, the analyses—described theoretically in previous chapters and illustrated by manual calculations in Appendixes B and C—can involve a major time- and resource-consuming effort, particularly if there are hundreds of users, thousands of jobs, and dozens of scenarios. Because of this, automation of the evaluation process is highly desirable.[3]

The objective of the examples presented in this chapter is to provide the reader with some indication of the power and diversity of the value approach in support of such decisions as:

1. What is the most effective scheduling rule?

[1]D. W. King and E. C. Bryant. *The Evaluation of Information Services and Products.* Washington, D.C., Information Resources Press, 1971.
[2]M. W. Mueller. "Time, Cost, and Value Factors in Information Retrieval." General Information Manual: Information Retrieval Systems Conference. White Plains, N.Y., International Business Machines Corporation, 1960. Brochure E 20-8040.
[3]The author has developed such an automated system which he has used to produce the results displayed and discussed in this chapter.

2. Is it better to allow random arrivals or to have a more controlled environment?

3. Should processing be done using an in-house or an outside service or both?

4. Should the current system be upgraded, downgraded, or retained?

THE AUTOMATED EVALUATION SYSTEM

The evaluation system uses job characteristics produced by the job stream generator shown in Figure 31. The job stream generator produces a randomized job stream, where the number of jobs, processing time, earliest start time, latest completion time, priority, maximum value, and so on, are determined by selecting values at random from specified probability distributions. These job characteristics make up a data base from which a series of analyzing programs operate, as shown in Figure 31.

In an actual rather than simulation mode, job characteristics are determined from results of a user survey and, for existing applications, from job accounting logs. The latter can provide such information as processing times, number of input and output operations, lines printed, disk residency, and so forth. For future applications, for which no such logs exist, the resource utilizations are obtained through questionnaires. The creation of a data base for an operational system is shown by the broken lines in the upper righthand corner of Figure 31.

Four examples of analyzing programs and the reports they generate are shown in Figure 31; others could be envisioned. The programs, labeled "Microsequencing Algorithms," "Environment," "Internal versus External," and "Speed/Capacity," generate Reports A, B, C, and D, respectively. The programs and reports are discussed in the next section.

MICROSEQUENCING ALGORITHMS

Four microsequencing rules were selected for evaluation: FCFS, SJF, priority, and c/t. The selected rules come from three major categories:

1. FCFS (first-come-first-served) rule—jobs are processed in the sequence in which they arrive for service.

2. SJF (shortest-job-first) rule—of those awaiting service, the

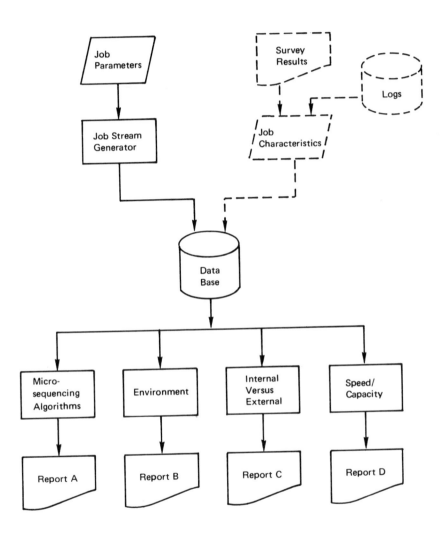

Figure 31 The automated evaluation system.

shortest job is the next to be processed when the service facility becomes available.

3. Value-oriented rules:

    a. Priority rule—of those awaiting service, the job with the highest prespecified priority is the next to be processed when the service facility becomes available.

    b. c/t Rule—of those awaiting service, the job (i) with the highest c/t ratio (c_i/t_i) is the next to be processed when the service facility becomes available, where c_i is the (constant) cost/rate of job i, and t_i is its expected processing time.

Based on assigned priorities of the jobs, job value functions are modified so that priority will affect sequencing under both priority and c/t rules and will affect individual jobs and aggregate values for all the microsequencing rules.

By varying the input parameters to the model, different arrival rates for potential jobs can be obtained. Two arrival densities, low and high, are used in Table 8, which is an example of Report A (see Figure 31). It can be seen, however, that all jobs that "arrive" are not necessarily processed, since their net values become nonpositive under the particular combination of arrival density, microsequencing rule, and processor speed. For example, for low arrival density and the FCFS rule, only 31 of the 53 potential jobs should be submitted. The 31 jobs would be processed for 16.76 hours of the 40-hour period under consideration. With job processing times varying between 0.1 and 1.2 hours, all 53 jobs could be processed within the total time frame, although this would mean processing 22 jobs that would yield nonpositive net values. Running the latter 22 jobs would further reduce the net values of some of the 31 jobs yielding positive net values, possibly to zero. The importance of the net value approach is its ability to eliminate worthless processing, which benefits the organization.

Continuing along the first line of Table 8, it is indicated that the average turnaround (processing plus wait time) is 1.70 hours for the FCFS rule, and the turnaround variance is 1.10 hours. On the next line, it is apparent that, for the SJF rule, average turnaround is reduced to 1.39 hours with a variance of only 0.69 hours. The priority and c/t rules' average turnaround and variance are similar to those of the FCFS rule. Note also that most jobs (34) are run under SJF; however, the SJF rule results in the lowest number of total processing hours (16.09 hours), whereas the c/t rule gives the highest.

If the rules are evaluated on traditional bases, the SJF rule provides

Table 8 System Performance Measures for Various Microsequencing Rules for Low and High Arrival Densities (Report A)

Arrival density	Microsequencing rule	Number of jobs run	Total processing (hours)	Average turnaround* (hours)	Variance of turnaround* (hours)	Total value lost† (money units)	Total net value† (money units)	Average net value† (money units)
Low (53 jobs)	FCFS	31	16.76	1.70	1.10	5,824	1,593	30.05
	SJF	34	16.09	1.39	0.69	5,659	1,758	33.16
	Priority	26	16.73	1.67	1.03	5,101	2,316	43.69
	c/t	30	17.46	1.68	1.24	4,469	2,948	55.62
High (127 jobs)	FCFS	47	22.29	2.04	1.21	15,298	1,838	14.47
	SJF	55	21.42	1.58	1.06	14,991	2,145	16.89
	Priority	42	22.79	1.96	1.30	14,887	2,249	17.71
	c/t	50	23.71	1.81	1.39	13,683	3,453	27.19

*For processed jobs.
†For all jobs available for submission.

Source: Adapted from C. W. Axelrod. "The Effective Use of Computer Resources." *Omega,* 4(3):329, August 1976. Reprinted by permission of Pergamon Press.

the best results on number of jobs run, average turnaround, and variance of turnaround, whereas the c/t rule yields the greatest number of processing hours. Clearly, the selection of the "best" rule becomes arbitrary.

The last three columns of Table 8 relate to the value aspects of schedules resulting from the microsequencing rules. In the model, the form of value hill used was that shown in Figure 27, where value is related to completion time from the time the job becomes available for processing to its deadline. Specifically, value is related linearly to completion time. Such simplifications are not required by the model— indeed, value hills of any degree of complexity can be used.

The loss in value and its complement, total net value, are shown for each microsequencing rule. The c/t rule clearly provides the greatest total net value and net value per available job.

The lower half of Table 8 contains equivalent information to the upper half for a higher arrival density. The relative values at the high arrival rate are consistent with the low arrival rate. It is apparent that the greater number of jobs available results in more jobs submitted and higher total net values; however, the average net value per job drops dramatically, indicating that the greater congestion of the high-density situation causes considerably more delay costs to be incurred by processed jobs.

ENVIRONMENT

In this example, two user environments are considered: random arrivals and arrivals by appointment.[4] The difference from the user's viewpoint is that, in the appointment system, he is guaranteed immediate service if he submits his job at a specific time. Turnaround time then becomes equivalent to processing time, since waiting time is eliminated, and the variance of turnaround time is reduced drastically to the variance of processing time. Of course, the implementation,

---

[4]B. Stevens. "Service Levels and the Service Level Matrix." *CMG Transactions,* *19*:3-2–3-18, March 1978. Stevens defines *demand batch* processing as "that portion of the workload whose performance is to be judged by turnaround time standards" and *scheduled batch* processing as "that portion of the workload that is to be evaluated on adherence to committed time deadlines." These two types of arrival streams are similar to the random and appointment environments. Stevens also differentiates between his two arrival stream categories and production and test (or development) jobs, stating that test jobs can be demand or scheduled batch, depending on the stage in the development cycle, and that production jobs fall into the scheduled batch category.

administration, and control of an appointment system will be much more costly than for a random arrival system in which users submit jobs as soon as they become available for processing. The gain in total net value (which is demonstrated in the next two paragraphs) must be set off against the cost of the appointment system, the latter being implemented only if there are demonstrable savings.

For the model, the shape of the value hills was modified to that shown in Figure 32. Here, the falloff in value relative to submission time is not as great as indicated in Figure 27 for the same completion time. This is meant to express the users' aversion to the relatively highly variable turnaround times that occur in the random arrival case and their preference for the lower turnaround variability of the appointment case. Thus, for example, a user may place as high a value on a later completion time known with certainty (as in the appointment case) as on an earlier completion time with great uncertainty (as in the random arrival case). For example, in Figure 32, $(X_1 + Y_1)$ and $(X_2 + Y_2)$ are equal; that is, they represent the same completion time. For the value hill in Figure 27, the same completion times would yield the same value. In Figure 32, they do not. Rather, the value realized is greater

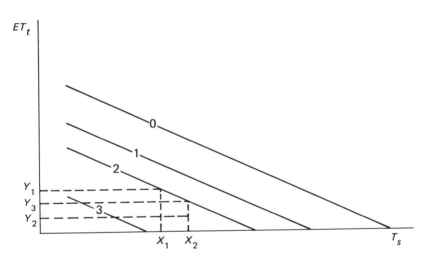

Source: C. W. Axelrod. "Effective Use of Computer Resources," p. 324. Reprinted by permission of Pergamon Press.

Figure 32 Value hill having different values for the same completion time.

for (X_2, Y_2). Conversely, submission at X_2 leads to the same value as (X_1, Y_1) if the completion time is $(X_2 + Y_3)$, where Y_3 is greater than Y_2. Basically, the difference between the value hill forms in Figure 32 and Figure 27 results from the implicit relationship between value and turnaround variance.

Using the appointment-oriented value hills yields the results in the lower half of Table 9, for the low arrival density case. These results can be compared with the random arrival case described in the previous section. The corresponding results are shown in the upper half of Table 9, which is a repetition of the upper half of Table 8. In the appointment case, many more jobs are processed (in fact, all available jobs are run under the c/t rule), and the net values realized are much greater for corresponding microsequencing rules. Whether or not an appointment system is justified depends on the job's value-sensitivity to turnaround variance and the cost of the appointment system itself.

INTERNAL VERSUS EXTERNAL

The process whereby users' computing needs are allocated among internal and external facilities was discussed in Chapter 5 and illustrated in Figure 11. Using the same job stream as that described in the previous sections as low arrival density and random arrival environment, the jobs were subjected to an FCFS microsequencing rule. Two experiments were run: In the first, only an external facility was available; in the second, both internal and external facilities were available. As will be shown, the net advantage (or disadvantage) of maintaining the internal system may be obtained by comparing the results of these two experiments.

External Only

In the first case, only external services were available, and the price per unit of processing and the queueing (or waiting) time were varied, as shown in the first two columns of Table 10. The price of zero is included for comparison purposes only and is not meant to indicate that free services were available. For each price, the waiting time is shown in half-hour increments up to the time for which no jobs would be processed. For example, 11 percent of the jobs would be run if the waiting time was 2.5 hours and the price $50 per unit. At a price of $100 per unit, no jobs would be run if the waiting time was 2.5 hours; but if

Table 9 System Performance Measures for Various Microsequencing Rules for Low Arrival Density in Two Macrosequencing Environments (Report B)

Macrosequencing environment	Microsequencing rule	Number of jobs run	Total processing (hours)	Average turnaround* (hours)	Variance of turnaround* (hours)	Total value lost† (money units)	Total net value† (money units)	Average net value† (money units)
Random arrivals	FCFS	31	16.76	1.70	1.10	5,824	1,593	30.05
	SJF	34	16.09	1.39	0.69	5,659	1,758	33.16
	Priority	26	16.73	1.67	1.03	5,101	2,316	43.69
	c/t	30	17.46	1.68	1.24	4,469	2,948	55.62
Appointment	FCFS	44	28.08	0.64	0.08	3,066	4,351	82.10
	SJF	51	29.80	0.58	0.07	1,838	5,579	105.26
	Priority	44	28.44	0.65	0.08	1,777	5,640	106.41
	c/t	53	31.96	0.60	0.08	1,317	6,100	115.09

*For processed jobs.
†For all jobs available for submission.

Source: Adapted from C. W. Axelrod. "Effective Use of Computer Resources." Reprinted by permission of Pergamon Press.

Table 10 The Effect of Price and Waiting Time on the Value of External Services—No Internal Service

Price (Dollars/ Unit)	Waiting Time (Hours)	Percentage of Jobs		Net Value to Total Available Value (Percent)
		Omitted	External	
0*	0.0	—	100	76
	0.5	—	100	57
	1.0	9	91	38
	1.5	34	66	23
	2.0	40	60	11
	2.5	53	47	3
	3.0	87	13	1
	3.5	87	13	0.6
	4.0	96	4	0.2
	4.5	96	4	0.2
	5.0	100	—	—
50	0.0	15	85	56
	0.5	26	74	39
	1.0	45	55	23
	1.5	64	36	12
	2.0	79	21	5
	2.5	89	11	0.2
	3.0	100	—	—
100	0.0	42	58	42
	0.5	55	45	27
	1.0	74	26	16
	1.5	83	17	8
	2.0	89	11	3
	2.5	100	—	—
150	0.0	57	43	34
	0.5	74	26	22
	1.0	83	17	12
	1.5	89	11	6
	2.0	94	6	2
	2.5	100	—	—
200	0.0	74	26	28
	0.5	79	21	18
	1.0	89	11	10
	1.5	89	11	5
	2.0	94	6	1
	2.5	100	—	—

*For comparison purposes only.

the waiting time was reduced to 2.0 hours, 11 percent of the jobs would be processed.

Obviously, the percentage of jobs run will vary relative to the price of processing and the waiting time, as indicated in column four of Table 10. Such a relationship is shown graphically in Figure 33, where the percentage of jobs run externally (which is the complement of the percentage of jobs omitted) is plotted against waiting time. Each curve represents a different price per unit of processing time (here, an hour), as noted. Although the curves are shown as smooth lines, the actual values in Table 10 are scattered about the lines. The graphs of Figure 33 provide approximate relationships which can be used to extrapolate the number of jobs run for prices or waiting times not given in Table 10.

Column five of Table 10 shows the percentage of the net value of jobs run to the total available value of jobs submitted. Note that, at zero price and zero waiting time, only 76 percent of the total available value is realized, the 24 percent value reduction being attributable to the delay due to processing time. In cases where external services are purchased for a price greater than zero, the net value is further reduced by the cost of services.

The relationships between percent of net value to total available value and waiting time are illustrated in Figure 34 for a series of prices. This kind of chart enables an administrator to evaluate services having prices falling between those shown and those with intermediate waiting times. For example, at a price of $85 per unit of processing time (here, an hour) and waiting time of 1.5 hours, about 10 percent of total available value will be realized.

External and Internal

Table 11 (Report C in Figure 31) is similar to Table 10, except that it includes an internal service for which no charge per unit of processing is made but for which waiting time delays are experienced, corresponding to the congestion of the internal system. For the external service, the waiting time is set at a fixed value independent of demand. The assumption of no charge for internal service corresponds to the assertion that the incremental costs of processing jobs are negligible relative to the fixed cost of the system. Of course, the model could be modified to include some internal pricing mechanism. The decision as to whether or not to have an internal system is based on a comparison of total net values on the corresponding lines of Tables 10 and 11. If the additional net value rendered by selecting the internal system exceeds the cost of that system, then an internal system should

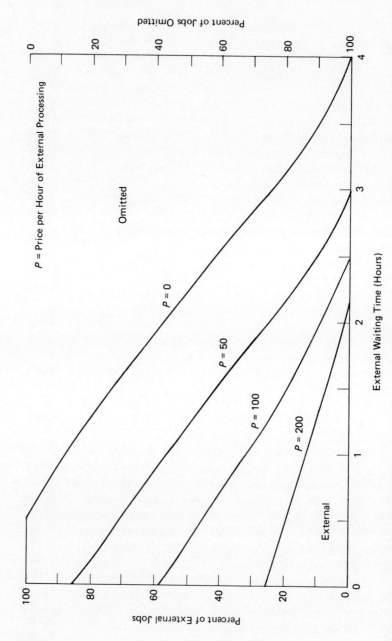

Figure 33 The effect of external waiting time and price per hour of processing on the percentage of jobs run externally (no internal service).

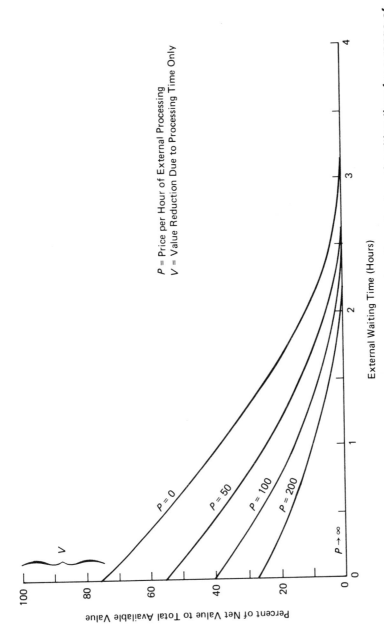

Figure 34 The percentage of total available value realized as a function of external waiting time for a range of prices (no internal service).

Table 11 The Effect of External Price and Waiting Time on Jobs Run Internally or Externally (Report c)

External Price (Dollars/ Unit)	External Waiting Time (Hours)	Percentage of Jobs			Net Value to Total Available Value (Percent)
		Omitted	Internal	External	
0*	0.0	—	26	79	76
	0.5	—	36	64	61
	1.0	10	45	45	49
	1.5	17	51	32	38
	2.0	23	51	26	30
	2.5	26	53	21	24
	3.0	42	56	2	22
	3.5	42	58	—	21
50	0.0	24	38	38	57
	0.5	19	47	34	47
	1.0	28	49	23	37
	1.5	34	55	11	30
	2.0	42	56	2	22
	2.5	42	58	—	21
100	0.0	28	49	23	50
	0.5	34	53	13	40
	1.0	34	53	13	34
	1.5	34	55	11	27
	2.0	42	56	2	22
	2.5	42	58	—	21
150	0.0	34	53	13	41
	0.5	34	53	13	35
	1.0	34	55	11	30
	1.5	34	55	11	25
	2.0	42	56	2	22
	2.5	42	58	—	21
200	0.0	34	53	13	38
	0.5	34	55	11	33
	1.0	34	55	11	28
	1.5	42	56	2	23
	2.0	42	56	2	22
	2.5	42	58	—	21

*For example, other in-house system.

be implemented. If the external system has price and waiting time characteristics that provide additional net value (above the cost of services), the external service should be used. If an internal system cannot be justified, an external service may still be beneficial if positive net value is obtained.

Columns three, four, and five in Table 11 show the percentages of jobs omitted, jobs run internally, and external services for different external price and waiting time combinations. These relationships are plotted in Figure 35. If the price of external services were infinite, 58 percent of the jobs would be run internally and the remaining 42 percent would be omitted. This is shown by the horizontal line labeled "$P \rightarrow \infty$," which is at 58 percent on the left vertical axis (percent of internal jobs) and at 42 percent on the right vertical axis (percent of jobs omitted, inverted scale). As the waiting time (horizontal axis) is reduced, a series of pairs of diverging lines forming envelopes develops from the "$P \rightarrow \infty$" line. The first pair of lines, labeled "$P = 0$," represents the boundaries of jobs run internally, externally, and omitted. The upper "$P = 0$" line gives the percent of jobs omitted, read from the right vertical axis; that is, at a waiting time of two hours, 23 percent of the jobs are omitted. The lower "$P = 0$" line gives the percent of jobs run internally, read from the left vertical axis, so that, at a waiting time of one hour, approximately 45 percent of the jobs are run internally. The difference between the upper and lower lines represents the percent of jobs run externally, so that for "$P = 0$" and a waiting time of 1.5 hours, the percent of external jobs is $(100 - 17 - 51)$, which equals 32 percent.[5] Figure 35 can be used for extrapolating intermediate prices and waiting times. It also provides a picture of the sensitivity of the systems to variations in the external services' parameters.

The relationship between the percent of net value to total available value versus external waiting time with an internal service available is illustrated in Figure 36. The chart is similar to Figure 34 except that the "$P \rightarrow \infty$" line is at a level of 21 percent, because at "$P \rightarrow \infty$" all jobs are run internally and they yield a positive net value.

In Figure 37, the curves of Figures 34 and 36 are compared for prices of zero and $200 per hour, respectively. Clearly, greater net values are realized if there is an internal service; however, as discussed earlier, an internal service is justified only if the net value difference exceeds the cost of such a system. As indicated in Figure 37, the net value difference (which is represented at any waiting time by the vertical distance between the upper and lower lines for the given price) varies both with waiting time and with price. Even for zero external waiting

[5]Note that, at zero price and zero external waiting time, Table 11 shows 26 percent of the jobs to be run internally. This occurs because the algorithm is to place jobs internally if the resulting net value is greater than *or equal to* the external net value. Consequently, in this case, if the internal computer is idle, the next available job will be assigned to it, otherwise it will be run externally. The net value attained is 76 percent, however, which is the same as the external only case of Table 10, which means that the internal system provides no additional value and cannot be justified at any price other than zero.

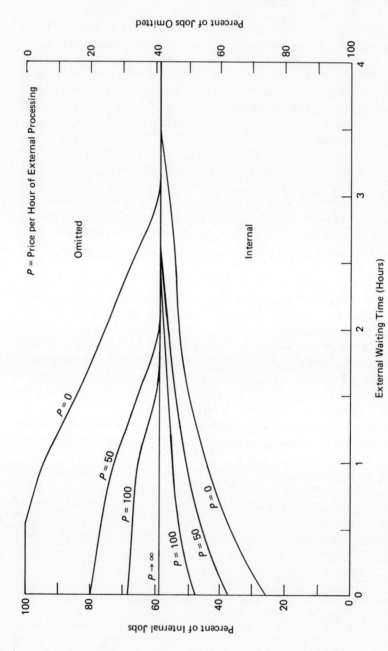

Figure 35 The effect of external waiting time and price per hour of processing on the percentage of jobs run externally and internally.

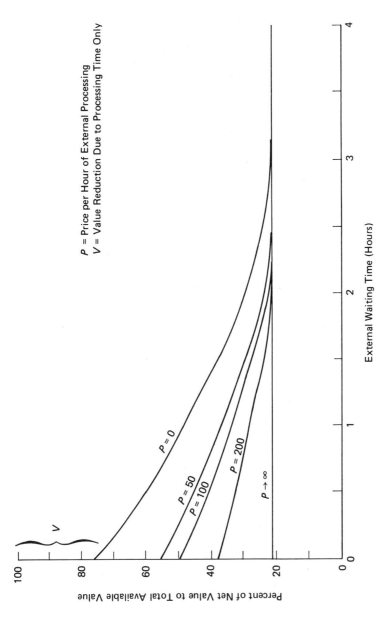

Figure 36   The percentage of total available value realized as a function of external waiting time for a range of prices (internal service used).

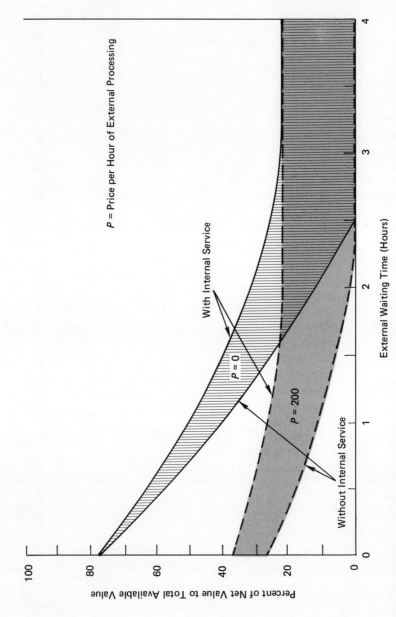

Figure 37   Comparison of percentage of total available value realized with and without internal service, for two prices.

time, an internal system may be justified if the external price is $200 per hour and the internal system costs less than 10 percent of the total available value.

SYSTEMS OF DIFFERENT SPEED

The upward spiral in the demand for computer services within an organization creates continual pressure to increase system capacity through bigger, faster, and more expensive machines. The resulting availability of more computing power will lead to an increase in load on the system as the improved service level encourages the implementation of new applications that previously were not feasible. Often, unrestrained growth in data processing will continue until money runs out.

How can it be determined when diminishing (or even negative) returns on the data-processing dollar have been reached? After all, the newer, faster machines usually are more cost-effective per computation or per unit of memory. Clearly, some measure of differentiation among systems is required that would reflect the real value of computing services to the organization and allow for variability both in type of application processed and in time. It should include all relevant costs as well as intangible costs and benefits.

Objective

In this section, a structure will be developed, within an organizational context, through which systems of different speeds can be compared both with respect to costs and to aggregate values of jobs processed. The objective is to select, from among systems with different processing speeds, the system that yields the highest value-to-cost ratio, as shown in Figure 38. This system is purchased if the value-to-cost ratio is higher than returns of other investments that the organization can make within its total budget and if the ratio is greater than one.[6]

Assumptions

The processing times of jobs run on systems of different speeds are assumed to bear the same linear relationship to each other.

[6]The decision regarding upgrading or downgrading also relates to whether or not any internal computer system should be maintained. This question was discussed earlier in this chapter in the "Internal Versus External" section.

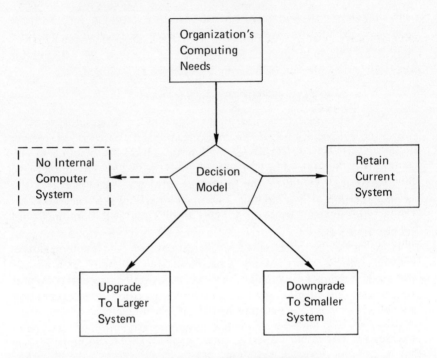

Figure 38   The upgrade/downgrade decision process.

Therefore, on a machine that is "twice as fast," all jobs will be processed in half the time. In reality, this would occur only if all components of the second machine (i.e., CPU, channels, memory, and so on) had the same speed relationship to the first machine, or if the resource requirements of all the jobs were the same.

Approach

Using the previous concept of the value hill, computer models of systems with different processing speeds were developed, and a series of job streams were run through the systems under several queueing disciplines (FCFS, SJF, priority, and c/t). For each scenario, the total value was obtained. The variations in total value with respect to processor speed, number of jobs, and microsequencing rules are illustrated in the following paragraph.

For a given number of jobs and the same microsequencing rule, processors of different speeds can be compared directly. Knowing the costs of the processors, a determination can be made of the most value-effective system. The model was run for a range of jobs in a given interval on the base processor, which had a speed of 1.0. Other processors, with speeds of 0.5 and 2.0, also were included.

Results

In Figure 39, derived from the results of Report D in Figure 31, the net value realized by the jobs that were processed is plotted against the total value of all jobs submitted. Although no example is shown, Report D is similar in format to Report A (Table 8).

If all jobs were processed immediately upon arrival at the facility, the results would fall along the "100 percent line" running at 45 degrees. The closer the points lie to this line, the higher the net-value-to-total-value ratio will be. Three shaded bands are shown, representing the ranges of the net-value-to-total-value ratios of the different scheduling rules. For speeds of 1.0 and 2.0, the c/t rule provides the upper limit of the band and the FCFS rule gives the lower limit, with the SJF and priority rules falling within the band. At the 0.5 speed, the points are too close together for this distinction to be made. Although the c/t rule still provides the upper bound in the latter case, the lower bound varies, that is, at some levels the SJF rule produces the poorest result. This is due, however, to the coarseness of the experiment and the close proximity of the points for the 0.5 speed.

While the differences due to speed are significant at high total values, the differences due to the scheduling rules also are considerable. Indeed, the FCFS rule for a machine of speed 2.0 is only slightly more effective than the c/t rule on a machine half the size. At some speed (perhaps 1.2), the slower machine under the c/t rule would be *more* effective than the 2.0 speed machine under FCFS. In order to eliminate the effect of the sequencing rule, the c/t rule is assumed for all speeds in the subsequent analysis, as shown in Figure 40.

Cost Considerations

It is well documented that the cost per computation decreases as the capacity or size of the computer increases, *ceteris paribus*. [7,8] Such a relationship is shown in Figure 41, where the total

---

[7] M. Phister, Jr. *Data Processing Technology and Economics*. Santa Monica, Calif., Santa Monica Publishing Company, 1976.
[8] W. F. Sharpe. *The Economics of Computers*. New York, Columbia University Press, 1969.

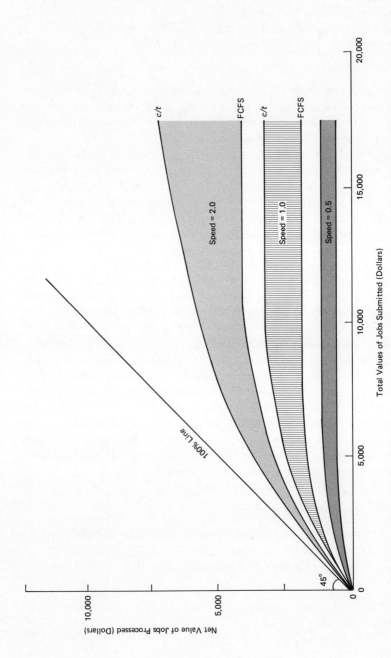

Figure 39 Net value as a function of total value for various processor speeds and for different scheduling rules.

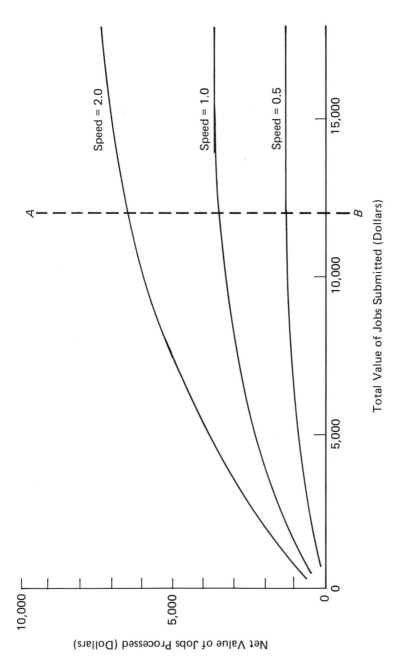

Source: C. W. Axelrod. "How Effective Is Your Computer?" *Infosystems, 26(2)*:52, February 1979. Reprinted by permission of Hitchcock Publishing Company.

Figure 40 Net value as a function of total value for various processor speeds for the *c/t* scheduling rule.

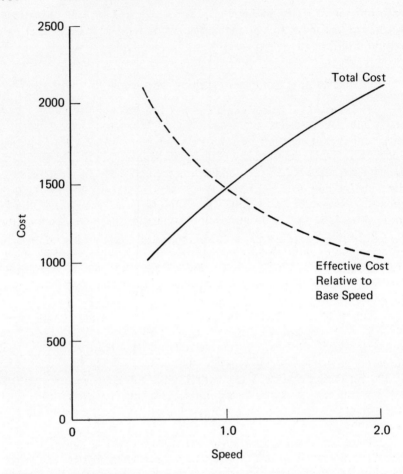

Figure 41   Cost versus speed.

cost (including equipment, maintenance, staff, and so on) is assumed to increase with speed according to the relationship

$$C = K\sqrt{S}$$

where C = cost of the computer system
S = speed of the system
K = some constant (here, equal to $1,500).

This is called Grosch's Law.[9] The effective cost, which is the cost per

[9]*Ibid.*, p. 315.

base unit of capacity (defined as 1.0 for a speed of 1.0), decreases according to $C/S = K/\sqrt{S}$, indicating economies of scale in cost per computation for the faster machines.

Bringing Costs and Values Together

Now that relationships have been obtained between speed and value and between speed and cost, how can the two be brought together? Assuming that the total value of jobs submitted is $12,000, under the c/t rule, net values will be approximately $6,500, $3,400, and $1,500 for speeds of 2.0, 1.0, and 0.5, respectively. This is illustrated by the vertical line AB in Figure 40. Similarly, net values for values submitted of $6,000 and $2,500, for example, may be obtained at the three processor speeds (Figure 40). Using the total costs at various speeds shown in Figure 41, and the net values at various speeds for different values submitted from Figure 40, the net value per unit cost at the various speeds may be calculated for the values submitted. The results are plotted for three values submitted ($12,000, $6,000, and $2,500) in Figure 42.

Examples using Figure 42 are as follows: If the value submitted is $12,000 and the required return is at least 50 percent (i.e., net value per unit cost = 1.5), then the cost per period will be at least $1,200 and the speed of the processor will be approximately 0.7. If the budget limit is $1,300 per period and the value submitted is $2,500, a negative return will be realized, suggesting that such a system is not a worthwhile investment. Even if the cost per period is $2,000, a return of only 8 percent will be realized.

If the value submitted is $6,000 per period and the budget limit is $1,200, the return will be 30 percent on a machine of speed 0.7. At a speed of 0.5, a negative return would result, even though the investment is reduced to $1,060.

By combining value, cost, budget, return, and speed considerations, the most effective computer system to satisfy users' needs and meet organizational constraints can be determined.

OTHER APPLICATIONS OF THE MODEL

This chapter examined some of the many applications of the value-based computer resource allocation model, particularly its use for selecting the optimal microsequencing rule, arrival environment, internal/external distribution of workload, and processing speed. These

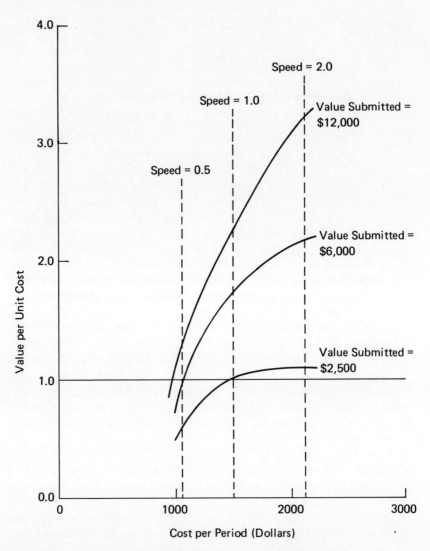

Figure 42 Net value per unit cost versus cost per period.

illustrative examples are not exhaustive—the model can be used for many other types of evaluation, such as the establishment of peak-load pricing rules, job priority determinations, new applications planning, and so on. For the peak-load pricing situation, an examination of the prior schedule results of the automated evaluation system will indicate times for which job value loss is high due to congestion. Peak-load prices can be introduced at these times and the resulting change in schedule observed. For the pricing scheme to be effective, the value of all jobs run—net of the prices charged—should show an increase. The priorities of jobs can be determined either by management fiat or by a method relying on scheduling data.[10] The model is used in the same mode as in the section on microsequencing algorithms earlier in this chapter. The effects of the priority rules can be evaluated and different priority job classes can be examined.

In new applications planning, the scheduling data for the applications are estimated and added to the data base. By comparing the results from the automated evaluation system, operating in any of the modes described in this chapter, both with and without the new applications, the effect of adding new jobs can be determined.

The model is not limited to computer systems: In Chapter 9, the potential application of these concepts to other fields is described.

[10]C. W. Axelrod. "Using Scheduling Data for Computer Resource Management." Presentation to the Northeast Region, Computer Measurement Group, New York, February 1979.

9
THE
IMPLICATIONS

The concepts and examples presented in this book have far-reaching implications for DP management, operations researchers, computer scientists, and investigators in other fields. The general conclusion is that, in typical organizational contexts, value-based computer allocation methods will lead to a higher total net value of computing than corresponding cost-based procedures. More specifically, the procedures provide DP management with an approach for improving the management of computer resources, the concepts introduce new avenues of potential investigation to researchers interested in the evaluation of computer-scheduling algorithms, and researchers from other disciplines might be encouraged to adapt some of the ideas to their particular requirements.

IMPLICATIONS FOR DP MANAGEMENT

Use and Extension of Concepts for Planning

Basically, the approach described in this book furnishes DP management with a structured system for computer resources allocation. For example, understanding that priority and pricing policies affect the shape of users' value hills, whereas turnaround-time (or response-time) schedules intersect with value hills but do not affect their shape, allows managers to separate priority and pricing decisions from capacity selection and sequencing rules. This separation simplifies the decision-making process by isolating independent deci-

164

sions, leading to improved decisions by focusing the manager's attention on specific items rather than on many conflicting factors.

These concepts also can be extended to other parts of the computer environment. In research and development activities, the greatest emphasis usually is placed on the computational stage, with input often prepared by the user and output directed uniquely to the user, frequently via a terminal or remote station. This contrasts with a batch production environment, where input preparation and the generation of output can be the major parts of the computer process. Distributed-processing systems and real-time transaction or terminal-oriented systems resemble the research environment, stressing the computational phase rather than preprocessing (input preparation) or postprocessing (output handling). In all of these cases, the response-time performance is paramount, and the approach described in this book is directly applicable.

In typical batch production installations, where the computational phase might be relatively minor in terms of resources, cost, and time expended, the same value-based planning methods can be used to advantage. For example, the use of value-based techniques can lead to better choices in deciding on the throughput capacity of the data entry (key-processing) facility, selecting a computer printer with the greatest effectiveness, determining whether data preparation should be done within the organization or by an outside service, and developing priority and sequencing rules for data preparation or the printer pool.

Recent product and service developments by computer and electronic equipment manufacturers on the one hand and communications service companies on the other hand portend major growth in the communications aspect of computers. Such data communication innovations include distributed-processing systems, in which the computational capability of the overall system resides in two or more separate computers tied together by communication links, and electronic mail, whereby information (which might originate in electronic or hard copy form) is transmitted over communication lines to the recipient, who receives hard copy or electronically (or magnetically) stored information accessible via a terminal. Word-processing systems, which began as typewriters with simple editing and retyping capabilities, are becoming more sophisticated and are acquiring many of the characteristics of computer systems, a trend which may well bring word processing under the purview of DP management.

Fundamentally, however, these new technologies possess the same characteristics as the computer systems described in preceding chapters; that is, they have users with time-sensitive job values vying for scarce, expensive, highly perishable (in terms of available resources) processing capacity. Consequently, the value-based techniques can be applied equally as well in advanced areas of data processing as in the traditional areas.

Convergence to Equilibrium

The stability of a system embodying the interaction between demand for services and computer turnaround time was considered in Chapter 3. In practice, it generally is not feasible to determine empirically the inherent feedback in such a system by taking measurements at different points in time (because demand usually fluctuates greatly over even short time intervals for most computer systems) or by measuring many systems at the same time (because few computer installations resemble one another in either demand or performance closely enough for meaningful survey work). Perhaps the only way to obtain some feel for the demand/turnaround relationships presented in Chapter 3 is by means of controlled testing, whereby the demands and turnaround times are artificially adjusted. This might enable management to predict, to some extent, the effects of real changes in the response times of computer systems by changing capacity, for example. The behavioral aspects of the interaction between users and turnaround are not well understood, which means that many decisions to increase capacity and improve turnaround tend to be ad hoc.

Most actual computer systems exhibit some degree of feedback behavior whether or not it is directly measurable. One example is the application of knowledge gained from one period to the next, assuming that the information relevant to the user is transferable between successive periods.[1] If the user discovers that the computer system is particularly busy at a certain time of day, he might choose to submit his work at another time, if possible. Otherwise, he might try to limit his demand by checking the program code more carefully in a test environment or by taking more time to ensure that the input data are accurate and complete for a production job, thereby reducing the need for rerunning the job.

---

[1]W. F. Sharpe. *The Economics of Computers*. New York, Columbia University Press, 1969, pp. 465–468. A similar procedure described by Sharpe is the scheme used by the Electricite de France Computing Center for the internal allocation of computer time among departments. In this case, four priorities were used, and the relative prices of the priority classes were revised every month. Since the users were given a maximum turnaround-time schedule for each priority level, the center was able to obtain a table showing the extent to which the anticipated turnaround times were met. The prices would then be revised in an attempt to bring about as close a similarity between desired and actual turnaround time as possible.

More Complicated Value Functions

It has been implicitly assumed that value functions are static to the extent that, once the relationship between value and the independent variables (e.g., submission time, turnaround time) has been established, it does not change. In practice, however, value functions may vary dynamically, because users refine their predicted values as they gain additional information; that is, the values of future jobs depend on the performance of current jobs. For example, if an early job requires more debugging runs than anticipated, the processing of subsequent jobs may become increasingly urgent as a deadline approaches. The inclusion of this dynamic aspect complicates both the empirical determination of the value functions and the rules for controlling the system.[2]

As with simpler forms of value functions, the efforts made to determine the forms of such functions with precision must be balanced against the benefits gained. For most practical purposes, the use of simpler forms of value functions, as discussed in Chapter 8, probably would be sufficient.

Use of Concepts in Operations

In the early 1970s, a number of software vendors began to develop computer packages—of varying degrees of sophistication and complexity—that were intended to provide operational schedules for jobs processed in a computer installation. These packages resemble in concept the planning package outlined in Chapter 8, except that, for the most part, they describe jobs and equipment in more detail. This is necessary to represent the operational environment more closely. For example, some packages divide jobs into steps, specify interdependencies between jobs, and often itemize particular resources (e.g., tape drives, disk drives, data files) used by each job step. The ways in which the scheduling packages handle the job and resource data range from simplistic to complex, as do the scheduling algorithms. These operational scheduling packages generally offer little flexibility for changing system parameters or for scheduling algorithms; consequently, they are somewhat limited as planning tools. Furthermore, the level of detail used by the packages requires that a major data-gathering effort must take place prior to running a schedule: Such an effort is necessary and worthwhile for an operational tool, but it seldom is justifiable for planning purposes.

[2]*Ibid.*, pp. 476–477.

The operational scheduling packages are primarily designed for batch production environments in which the bulk of job processing follows regular periodic cycles. Jobs submitted at irregular intervals, unanticipated requests for service, and jobs entered from remote locations (remote batch or time sharing) generally are considered nonschedulable, but sometimes they can be handled by assigning resources for blocks of time.

For a complex operational environment, in which hundreds of interrelated jobs with strict deadlines are processed each day, such scheduling packages provide invaluable assistance to computer operations management. Another important feature of some scheduling packages is their adaptability for multiprogramming—the concurrent processing of a number of jobs within the computer itself—by assigning different resources to different jobs at the same time. For example, if one job is in the central processor, another might be reading data from a tape, and so on, with all the tasks taking place simultaneously. Multiprogramming has the effect of increasing the utilization of different parts of the computer configuration, at the cost of increasing computer-operating overhead. Most computers (except for the smallest ones) contain supervisory systems that control the movement and processing of jobs as they pass through the computer and manage the available resources (i.e., the processor, peripheral units, and so on). In more sophisticated systems, jobs can be assigned priorities that may remain static or change dynamically with either the time elapsed or the amount of processing received.

Chapter 8 presented an illustration of priority scheduling, where jobs were presumed to be processed sequentially. In a multiprogramming environment, however, jobs compete against one another for access to various parts of the computer configuration. It is possible, in some cases, to establish preferential access to all or parts of the system, based on a prespecified priority and job class hierarchy. Such sophisticated resource and job management has many potential benefits in theory, but the establishment of a suitable priority structure is by no means trivial and, generally, is beyond the scope of operations management. Data-processing general management, on the other hand, usually is not familiar with the complexity of the internal priority systems of computers; the kind of scheduling information described herein can be helpful, as can the basic input data required for commercial scheduling.

Parameters such as earliest start time (submission time), desired completion time, and processing time can be used to derive an "urgency factor" for jobs.[3] Jobs then may be assigned priorities, based on their relative urgency in a multiprogramming environment. In practice, it has been found that such an approach is able to identify time-critical jobs successfully.

Generally, the input parameters for operational scheduling packages are single-valued (e.g., start time) rather than functional in form (as for a value hill). Often, it is difficult to obtain even single-valued descriptors; however, the more complex value functions are much more meaningful in operational practice and in planning. For example, a user may supply an earliest start time and latest desired completion time for a job, but the weights to be given such times can vary widely. The difference between "It would be nice to get it back some time tomorrow" and "I have to have it by 3 p.m. or we shall lose a $5 million account" is not conveyed by single-valued parameters, but would be if value functions were specified.

IMPLICATIONS FOR THE COMPUTER RESEARCHER

Although much work is being done on computer scheduling and is written up with regularity in the operations research and computer literature,[4] most of these analyses are based on somewhat simplifying assumptions with respect to user behavior, the cost of delays, and the criteria for evaluating schedules.[5] The structure developed in this book can provide researchers with new avenues of productive endeavor, as will be described in the following sections.

Empirical Determination of Value Functions

While it might be the responsibility of DP management to determine specific relationships between the values of jobs and other factors for a particular situation, it is the researcher's responsibility to develop better techniques (e.g., surveys, regression analysis, and induc-

---

[3]C. W. Axelrod. "Using Scheduling Data for Computer Resource Management." Presentation to the Northeast Region, Computer Management Group, New York, February 1979.

[4]See, for example, H. J. Greenberg, D. Heyman, and R. Van Slyke, eds., "Operations Research/Computer Sciences Interface," *Operations Research*, 26:685–935, September–October 1978.

[5]Even though the assumptions may be relatively simple, the derivations of mathematical expressions can be very complex. Indeed, if the assumptions were not kept simple, many formulations would not be tractable analytically.

tion) for management to follow. Also, the primary factors that might affect value, and possible secondary and tertiary effects, should be researched. Proceeding a step further, it may be possible to classify job value functions by type of user, industry, type of application, and so on, in order to simplify the data-gathering process and to validate results of user surveys for specific computer centers.

Derivation of Scheduling Rules

Of all the areas examined by computer researchers, perhaps the most abundant is that of scheduling algorithms. Not only can the value function concepts form the basis of a whole new series of value-oriented scheduling disciplines, they can be used to develop value-oriented criteria for evaluating scheduling rules, computer capacities, and job submission policies, as was done in Chapter 8 to some degree.

Behavioral Aspects

Perhaps the least understood part of computer resource allocation systems is the behavioral or motivational aspect. Further research in this area would be most revealing. For example, users may respond to turnaround-time information in more complex ways than described in Chapter 3, in that they might attempt to *anticipate* how the computer system will respond in the future and modify their behavior to suit the anticipated response rather than the actual response. The user might attempt to second-guess other users and to manipulate the system to better suit his needs, possibly by adjusting the priority of his jobs or breaking large jobs into several small ones. A game-theoretic model could be developed to reflect such behavior.

Conversely, the researcher might develop strategies for the computer center to induce desirable responses from users.[6] Such strategies might resemble the false feedback approach described in Chapter 3 and might be based on the simple response mechanism presented in that chapter, or they might become very complex game-theoretic formulations.

---

[6] For an approach to inducing computer users to provide their true value functions, see R. J. Dolan, "Priority Pricing Models for Congested Systems," Working Paper Series No. 7710, Rochester, N.Y., Graduate School of Management, University of Rochester, 1977. Mimeographed. For an extension of the working paper to a general service facility, see R. J. Dolan, "Incentive Mechanisms for Priority Queuing Problems," *Bell Journal of Economics*, 9:421–436, Autumn 1978.

The above research, hopefully, would provide conditions for convergence to equilibrium for the interactions between users and the computer center. This would be invaluable for system sizing and performance standard specifications.

IMPLICATIONS FOR OTHER AREAS OF RESEARCH

Throughout this book, references have been made to other fields. In this section, examples are presented of possible fruitful extensions of the concepts derived in a specific computer environment to noncomputer situations that share some of the characteristics of the computer-effectiveness model.

Transportation

The transportation field is analogous to computers in many ways. Travelers, whether they are in automobiles using highways or are passengers on aircraft, trains, or buses, demand service from a facility which has limited capacity. Actually, there are two constraints on the travelers: first, the capacity of the vehicle and, second, the capacity of the medium in or on which the vehicle travels—a highway, shipping lane, air lane, or railroad track. The means of managing the media, such as traffic lights, air traffic control, and railroad signals, can affect priorities on vehicles using the travel media. In addition, the staging areas, such as airports, railroad stations, docks, and highway toll booths, affect the capacity of the entire system and may, in some cases, be limiting factors.

In all of these situations, planning involves the determination of capacities, priorities, scheduling, and pricing. Users of transportation systems often are subject to delays that might be caused by congestion or adverse controlling rules (or poor management). Such delays result in costs that vary among travelers for a given amount of delay and over time. These costs can be expressed in terms of value functions, and the same concepts and analyses can be applied as for computer jobs.

Job-Shop Scheduling

A computer center is, in essence, a job shop, with jobs entering the center and receiving service from a series of stations (e.g., data preparation, computer processing, output production).

Elmaghraby differentiates job shops from other manufacturing facilities that produce standard stock items by explaining that job shops service customer-originating demands for a variable product mix.[7] Coffman combines consideration of computer scheduling and job-shop scheduling into a single volume.[8] All of the concepts presented in this book, apart from those that clearly pertain only to computers, can be adapted to the job shop.

Land Use

In urban planning, the trade-off between the cost of assigning land for a particular use, such as roads, and the congestion arising from not using the land in such a manner requires the planner to determine the relationship between values of alternative uses and delays due to congestion.

Appointment Systems

Appointments are common in business and in professional/client situations. It is presumed that, by making arrivals deterministic rather than random, appointments can reduce waiting time, thereby saving time and money for both the server and the served. In Chapter 8, it was assumed that customers are less sensitive to when they are served if an appointment has been made (and kept) than they would be in a random arrival situation; however, the value loss incurred if the appointed service initiation time is delayed will be much greater than for random service.

The appointment situation becomes even more complex when the possibility of the customer being late is included, since then the server is delayed at some cost. The trade-off between the customers' and server's value functions raises some interesting strategy questions.

CONCLUSION

Clearly, potential extensions of the computer-effectiveness concepts are many and varied, both within and outside the computer field, and for management and research.

---

[7]S. E. Elmaghraby. *The Design of Production Systems*. New York, Reinhold, 1966, p. 289.
[8]E. G. Coffman, Jr., ed. *Computer and Job-Shop Scheduling Theory*. New York, John Wiley and Sons, 1976.

APPENDIX A

THE "CAPACITIES" OF TWO DIFFERENT COMPUTER INSTALLATIONS WITH THE SAME THROUGHPUT

Two computer installation configurations will be considered: System A, consisting of one computer that processes an average of n jobs per unit time, and System B, consisting of two smaller computers, each of which processes an average of $n/2$ jobs per unit time. Both systems provide the same average throughput of n jobs per unit time. It is assumed that jobs arrive at random, with the average arrival rate λ. The interval of time between two successive arrivals is therefore a random variable with an exponential distribution and mean value $1/\lambda$.[1] Also, the processing times of jobs are assumed to be independent values from a fixed exponential distribution with mean $1/n$ for System A and $2/n$ for each of the computers in System B. The traffic intensity, ρ, is defined to be the ratio of the mean service time of a job to the mean interval between successive arrivals for the single-server case. The denominator of ρ is multiplied by the number of servers in multiple-server examples, where all servers are identical, that is:

$$\rho_A = \frac{\lambda}{n} \text{ and } \rho_B = \frac{\lambda \times 2}{2 \times n} = \frac{\lambda}{n} ,$$

[1]D. R. Cox and W. L. Smith. *Queues*. London, Methuen, 1961.

173

Table 12   Comparison Between Systems of Various Queue Characteristics

| System | Queue Characteristics | | Average Number of Jobs in the System |
	p_o	p_n	
A	$1 - \rho_A$	$\rho_A^n(1 - \rho_A)$	$\dfrac{\rho_A}{(1 - \rho_A)}$
B	$\dfrac{1 - \rho_B}{1 + \rho_B}$	$\dfrac{2\rho_B^n(1 - \rho_B)}{1 + \rho_B}$	$\dfrac{2\rho_B}{(1 - \rho_B^2)}$

where ρ_A is the traffic intensity for System A, and ρ_B is the traffic intensity for System B. Let p_i denote the probability that there are i jobs in the system under steady-state conditions. Therefore, for Systems A and B, the p_i and the average number of jobs in the system may be expressed as fairly simple functions of the traffic intensity, as indicated in Table 12.[2]

The values ρ_A and ρ_B are equal for identical arrival distributions since the overall service rates of both systems are the same. Consequently, the various characteristics in Table 12 can be compared directly. For example, p_o, the probability that the system is empty, differs by a factor of $1/(1 + \rho_B)$, which is close to unity for low values of traffic intensity but approaches 0.5 as ρ_B approaches unity.[3] Values of the characteristics in Table 12 for a range of ρ are given in Table 13.

Table 13 highlights significant differences between the two systems. For values of ρ below 0.2, the average number of jobs in System A is about half that in System B. At this level, the systems are empty much of the time, so processing time accounts for most of the time a job spends in the system. Each job consequently tends to be in System B twice as long as in System A. For values of ρ above 0.8, emphasis is shifted to the waiting time, which is approximately the same in both systems, since the throughputs are equal. The average number of jobs is approximately 0.5 greater for System B than for System A at high

[2]For proof of the single-server case, see *ibid.*, pp. 39–42; for proof of the multiple-server case, see *ibid.*, pp. 45–46.
[3]Note that, for a stable system, $0 < \rho < 1$.

values of ρ because of the higher expected processing time for each job processed through System B; that is, in a congested system, there usually will be two jobs in service in System B versus one in System A, giving a slightly higher average number of jobs in System B. The percentage difference between the average number of jobs in the two systems becomes less significant as the traffic intensity approaches unity.

Since each job takes twice as long to process in System B, the probability that there are no jobs in that system will intuitively be greater for System A. The ratio of the probability of no jobs in System A to that of System B varies from just above 1 for low values of ρ to almost 2 for high values of ρ, because System A processes jobs at twice the rate of one machine in System B, which is the significant factor as the systems become congested.

Table 13   Various Queue Characteristics Evaluated over a Range of ρ

Traffic Intensity	Average Number of Jobs in the System		Probability of No Jobs in the System	
	System A	System B	System A	System B
0.1	0.111	0.210	0.9	0.82
0.2	0.250	0.416	0.8	0.67
0.3	0.429	0.659	0.7	0.54
0.4	0.667	0.953	0.6	0.43
0.5	1.000	1.333	0.5	0.33
0.6	1.500	1.875	0.4	0.25
0.7	2.333	2.745	0.3	0.18
0.8	4.000	4.450	0.2	0.11
0.9	9.000	9.480	0.1	0.05
0.98	49.000	49.495	0.02	0.01

Traffic Intensity	Probability that One Job Is in System B	Probability that One Server Is Free in System B
0.1	0.164	0.984
0.2	0.268	0.938
0.3	0.324	0.864
0.4	0.344	0.774
0.5	0.333	0.667
0.6	0.300	0.550
0.7	0.252	0.432
0.8	0.176	0.286
0.9	0.095	0.148
0.98	0.020	0.030

In the lower half of Table 13, the probability that one job is in System B is indicated. By adding this to the probability that there are no jobs in System B, the probability that one machine of System B is free for a range of values of ρ is obtained. Compared to System A, for which the equivalent measure is the probability of no jobs in the system, the probability that a job will be serviced immediately upon entering the system is higher for System B, especially at high traffic intensities. Even though, on the average, the number of jobs in A is less than in B at the same ρ, the chance of immediate service is higher for B.

CONCLUSION

Although the "throughputs" of Systems A and B are equal, their queueing characteristics are different. These differences vary with the degree of congestion in the system. Consequently, the comparative desirability of systems will depend on the expected congestion level of the system, as well as on such factors as certain hardware costs.

From a practical viewpoint, System B provides one machine as backup in the event of a single machine failure. Under such circumstances, 50 percent of the processing capacity of System B remains available, whereas with System A, all processing capability is lost in the event of a failure. If all the machines are equally reliable, the probability of the two machines in System B being incapacitated is much less than the probability of System A being down.

APPENDIX B

ILLUSTRATIVE EXAMPLE OF INTERNAL/EXTERNAL JOB ASSIGNMENT[1]

In this example, jobs to be processed within a given period are considered, and it is assumed that their value functions are insensitive to the time of submission within the period, varying only with expected waiting time, ET_w.[2] This assumption yields value hills as shown in Figure 24.

Letting v_i (ET_w) represent the value function of job i,[3] value functions are arbitrarily assigned to the nine jobs as follows:

$$\left.\begin{array}{rcl} v_1(ET_w) & = & 50 - ET_w \\ v_2(ET_w) & = & 20 \\ v_3(ET_w) & = & 60 - 10ET_w^{.05} \\ v_4(ET_w) & = & 65 - 0.5ET_w \\ v_5(ET_w) & = & 40 - 4ET_w \\ v_6(ET_w) & = & 120 - 3ET_w - 0.5ET_w^{0.5} \\ v_7(ET_w) & = & 70 - 0.02ET_w^3 \\ v_8(ET_w) & = & 160 - ET_w - ET_w^2 \\ v_9(ET_w) & = & 280 - ET_w^2 - 50ET_w^{0.5} \end{array}\right\} \quad (A)$$

[1]Adapted from C. W. Axelrod. "The Effective Assignment of User Demand Among Computer Services." *CMG Transactions, 15*:3-28–3-36, March 1977. By permission of The Computer Measurement Group, Inc.

[2]In the previous specifications of the model, value was related to turnaround time rather than waiting time, where turnaround time is processing time plus waiting time. For a system of specific capacity, it is contended that the value function is more sensitive to waiting time than processing time, since the latter is known in advance and does not vary

177

Users may run jobs either internally or externally. The external waiting time is constant throughout the period at a value of 3 time units and is independent of the level of demand from internal users.[4]

The Internal Waiting Time

For a computer facility of fixed capacity, the expected waiting time increases at an accelerated rate with higher demand per period. For random arrivals and exponential service, the expected number of jobs in the system is low when the mean interarrival time is well above the mean service time. As the mean interarrival time approaches the mean service time, the expected waiting time rises rapidly, tending towards infinity as the traffic intensity (i.e., mean arrival rate divided by mean service rate) approaches unity.

In this example, the arrival pattern is random, and the service times are exponentially distributed. It is assumed that the waiting time can be estimated when the number of jobs that are allocated to the internal facility is known and is expressed by the relationship[5]

$$ET_w = \frac{N}{k - N},$$

where ET_w is the expected waiting time, N is the number of jobs run internally, and k is a constant which is greater than N for all values of N. If k is equal to 10, then the expected internal waiting time takes the

---

over time. Consequently, to simplify the illustration, value is related directly to waiting time in this example.

[3]Each job in this example should be considered to be a group of jobs or a job stream, the members of which arrive randomly throughout the interval. The value of the job stream depends on the average expected turnaround of its members.

[4]It is assumed that, for a given job, the external system requires the same processing time as the internal system.

[5]See W. F. Sharpe, *The Economics of Computers,* New York, Columbia University Press, 1969, p. 461. Sharpe gives the relationship for expected waiting time (ET_w) as

$$\left(\frac{p}{1-p}\right)\frac{1}{\mu},$$

where $p = \lambda/\mu$, λ is the number of jobs submitted per unit time, μ is the number of jobs serviced per unit time, and p is the proportion of the time the processor is utilized. The relationship can be simplified by setting $\mu = 1$, giving waiting time as $\lambda/1 - \lambda$. Substituting N/k for λ gives the equation

$$ET_w = \frac{N}{k - N},$$

where k is a constant related to the capacity of the system and N is the number of jobs submitted. This formulation expresses the number of arrivals as a fraction of the capacity of the system.

values shown in Table 14 for various N. The same results are plotted in Figure 43.

The Total Value of Jobs Processed

The value of a job is obtained by substituting the expected waiting time into its value function in the list of relationships on page 177. For example, if job I is run externally, the expected turnaround time will be 3 time units, and its value will be 47 value units. If, on the other hand, job I is run internally with four other jobs, its expected waiting time is 1 time unit (see Table 14, for $N = 5$), and its value is 49 value units.

Table 15 indicates the values of all job streams at all feasible internal and external expected waiting times. The difference in value between running a particular job internally and externally is tabulated for all feasible expected waiting times in Table 16.

To obtain the *efficient bound* for any specific combination of internal and external processing, those jobs for which the excess value of internal over external processing is the greatest are selected for internal processing. Conversely, those jobs for which the excess value of external over internal processing is the least are selected for internal processing where the external waiting time is less than the internal time. For example, if one of the nine jobs is run internally and the other eight are run externally, the latter will be subjected to an expected waiting time of 3 time units, whereas the job that is run internally will have a waiting time of only 0.1 time units. Table 15 provides the values of all jobs for expected waiting times of 0.1 and 3 time units. In Table

Table 14   The Relationship Between the Number of Jobs Run Internally and the Expected Internal Waiting Time

Number of Jobs Run Internally (N)	Expected Internal Waiting Time (ET_w)
1	0.1
2	0.2
3	0.4
4	0.7
5	1.0
6	1.5
7	2.3
8	4.0
9	9.0

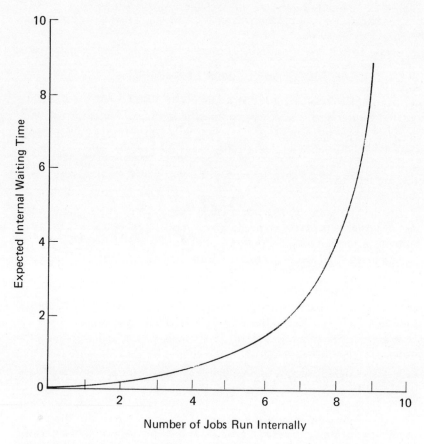

Source: C. W. Axelrod. "How Effective Is Your Computer?" *Infosystems, 26*(2):52, February 1979. Reprinted by permission of Hitchcock Publishing Company.

Figure 43   The internal congestion delay function.

16, the additional value accruing to each job, if it is run internally rather than externally, is shown in the first column of numbers ($ET_{ir} = 0.1$). The maximum value difference is 79.8 for job *9*. Thus, according to the rule for determining the efficient bound, jobs *1–8* should be run externally and job *9* should be run internally, resulting in a total value of 799.7 (see Table 17). The efficient bound of total values for all feasible combinations is tabulated in Table 17, and is represented by the total value curve of Figure 44. The maximum total value of 805.5 occurs when three jobs are run internally and six jobs, externally.

Table 15 Values of Jobs for all Feasible Waiting Times

Job Number	Expected Waiting Time									
	0.1	0.2	0.4	0.7	1.0	1.5	2.3	3.0*	4.0	9.0
1	49.9	49.8	49.6	49.3	49.0	48.5	47.7	47.0	46.0	41.0
2	20.0	20.0	20.0	20.0	20.0	20.0	20.0	20.0	20.0	20.0
3	51.1	50.8	50.5	50.2	50.0	49.8	49.6	49.4	49.3	48.9
4	65.0	64.9	64.8	64.7	64.5	64.3	63.9	63.5	63.0	60.5
5	39.6	39.2	38.4	37.2	36.0	34.0	30.8	28.0	24.0	4.0
6	119.5	119.2	118.5	117.5	116.5	114.9	112.3	110.1	107.0	91.5
7	70.0	70.0	70.0	70.0	70.0	69.9	69.8	69.5	68.7	55.4
8	159.9	159.8	159.4	158.8	158.0	156.3	152.4	148.0	140.0	70.0
9	264.2	257.6	248.2	237.7	229.0	216.5	198.9	184.4	164.0	49.0

*For external facility.

Table 16 Differences in Value Between Internally and Externally Run Jobs for All Feasible Expected Waiting Times

Job Number	Expected Waiting Time									
	0.1	0.2	0.4	0.7	1.0	1.5	2.3	3.0*	4.0	9.0
1	2.9	2.8	2.6	2.3	2.0	1.5	0.7	0.0	−1.0	−6.0
2	0.0	0.0	0.0	0.0	0.0	0.0	0.0	0.0	0.0	0.0
3	1.7	1.4	1.1	0.8	0.6	0.4	0.2	0.0	−0.1	−0.5
4	1.5	1.4	1.3	1.2	1.0	0.8	0.4	0.0	−0.5	−3.0
5	11.6	11.2	10.4	9.2	8.0	6.0	2.8	0.0	−4.0	−24.0
6	9.4	9.1	8.4	7.4	6.4	4.8	2.2	0.0	−3.1	−18.6
7	0.5	0.5	0.5	0.5	0.5	0.4	0.3	0.0	−0.8	−14.1
8	11.9	11.8	11.4	10.8	10.0	8.3	4.4	0.0	−8.0	−78.0
9	79.8	73.2	53.8	53.3	44.6	32.1	14.5	0.0	−20.4	−135.4

*For external facility.

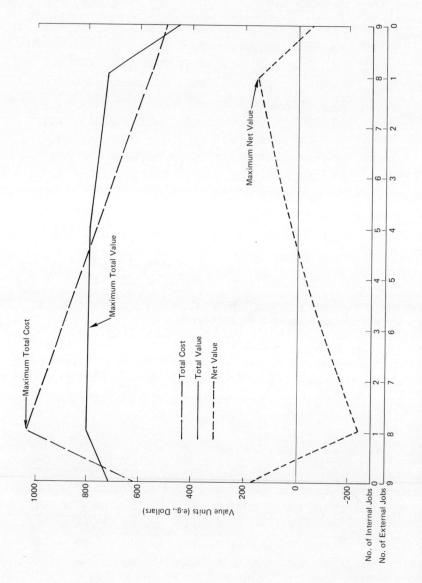

Figure 44 Values and costs for all feasible internal/external combinations.

Table 17 The Total Value of Jobs Processed for Feasible Internal/External Combinations

	Jobs Run Internally									
	0	1	2	3	4	5	6	7	8	9
	Jobs Run Externally									
Job Number	9	8	7	6	5	4	3	2	1	0
1	[47.0]	[47.0]	[47.0]	[47.0]	[47.0]	49.0	48.5	47.7	46.0	41.0
2	[20.0]	[20.0]	[20.0]	[20.0]	[20.0]	[20.0]	[20.0]	[20.0]	20.0	20.0
3	[49.4]	[49.4]	[49.4]	[49.4]	[49.4]	[49.4]	[49.4]	[49.4]	49.3	48.9
4	[63.5]	[63.5]	[63.5]	[63.5]	[63.5]	[63.5]	64.3	63.9	63.0	60.5
5	[28.0]	[28.0]	[28.0]	38.4	37.2	36.0	34.0	30.8	24.0	4.0
6	[110.1]	[110.1]	[110.1]	[110.1]	117.5	116.5	114.9	112.3	107.0	91.5
7	[69.5]	[69.5]	[69.5]	[69.5]	[69.5]	[69.5]	[69.5]	69.8	68.7	55.4
8	[148.0]	[148.0]	159.8	159.4	158.8	158.0	156.3	152.4	140.0	70.0
9	[184.4]	264.2	257.6	248.2	237.7	229.0	216.5	198.9	[184.4]	49.0
Total Value	719.9	799.7	804.9	805.5	800.6	790.9	773.4	745.2	722.4	440.3

Key: [ ] Job is run externally.

The fixed cost of having the internal computer facility available throughout the period is assumed to be 500 money units, and the variable costs of internal computing are negligible. It is further assumed that the cost per job of running jobs externally is 67 money units. The total cost curve for all feasible internal/external combinations is shown in Figure 44.

By subtracting the total cost from the total value for all combinations, the net value curve is obtained, as indicated in Figure 39. The maximum net value—155.4 money units—occurs when eight jobs are run internally and one is run externally. It should be noted that this is a different combination from that of total value maximization, which occurs when three jobs are run internally, or from that of total cost minimization, which takes place when all jobs are run internally.

APPENDIX C

ILLUSTRATIVE EXAMPLE OF MACROSEQUENCING

General Procedure

In Chapter 6, it was assumed that the value of a job is predominantly dependent on the submission time of the job and the expected turnaround time. The value of job i may be expressed as $v_i(T_s, ET_t)$, where T_s is the submission time and ET_t is the expected turnaround time. Furthermore, the ET_t schedule confronting job i is a function of T_s, that is, $ET_t = f_i(T_s)$. By substituting the ET_t schedule in the value function, the value of job i may be expressed as a function of T_s only, that is,

$$\text{Value of job } i = v_i[T_s, f_i(T_s)] = u_i(T_s).$$

The user will submit the job at that T_s which provides the highest value. If $u_i(T_s)$ is continuously differentiable with respect to T_s, then the conditions for a maximum are

$$\frac{\partial u_i(T_s)}{\partial T_s} = 0$$

$$\frac{\partial^2 u_i(T_s)}{\partial T_s^2} < 0, \text{ in the neighborhood of } T_s^*,$$

where T_s^* is a value of T_s that satisfies the first condition. Of course, the function u_i may have more than one local maximum, in which case the

184

largest maximum over all T_s is the global maximum. If the value function is discrete, then the maximum value is obtained by evaluating u_i over all values of T_s and selecting the T_s that gives the greatest u_i.

In this example, the objective is to maximize the average net value per unit time, from the start of processing the first job until the end of processing the last job. This assumes that there are direct costs associated with the time during which the computer is "up," and that the computer remains "up" throughout the whole period. Note that, if the only costs of significance are independent of the number of jobs processed per unit time, the objective becomes that of maximizing the total net value of all jobs. These objectives may be the same if there is no idle time between jobs, and if all the available computing time is fully utilized.

Assumptions

Job submissions take place at discrete times, and the jobs are serviced according to the first-come-first-served rule. If two jobs arrive at the same time, the shorter one is run first. If more than two jobs arrive simultaneously, they are run in order of increasing expected processing time. The goals of users and the organization are consistent, so that value functions represent the utilities of jobs to both users and the organization.

The Analytical Procedure

This example considers four jobs (a, b, c, and d), with the following respective value functions:

$$v_a(T_s, ET_t) = 100 - 10 [(T_s - 6)^2 + (ET_t - ET_{t,a}^{min})^2]^{0.5}$$
$$v_b(T_s, ET_t) = 120 - 12 (ET_t - ET_{t,b}^{min})$$
$$v_c(T_s, ET_t) = 80 - 4 [(T_s - 3) + (ET_t - ET_{t,c}^{min})] \text{ for } T_s \geq 3$$
$$v_d(T_s, ET_t) = 140 - 8(ET_t - ET_{t,d}^{min}) \text{ for } T_s = 5$$
$$= 0, \text{ otherwise}$$

The term $ET_{t,i}^{min}$ is the minimum expected turnaround time that job i would experience if it entered service immediately upon arrival and is equivalent to its processing time, assuming that there are no variations in setup times due to successive jobs of different types. If the computer facility is of constant configuration over the relevant time period, $ET_{t,i}^{min}$ does not change over time. The term $ET_t - ET_{t,i}^{min}$ is the expected queueing time of job i. Users are assumed to respond to the expected waiting time in the queue, ET_w. If a larger, faster computer is installed, the processing time of job i is reduced.

In this example, jobs have the following processing times:

Processing time of job a = 2 time units
Processing time of job b = 5 time units
Processing time of job c = 4 time units
Processing time of job d = 3 time units

Since the processing times are known, the expected waiting times are deterministic for given times of submission.

The ET_w schedule of a job is defined as the relationship between expected waiting time and time. In this example, the waiting time schedule of any job depends on the times at which the other three jobs are submitted. The ET_w schedule for any job is ascertained by considering the waiting time that the job will experience at all relevant values of T_s, given that the other three jobs are submitted at given times.

The Initial Round of the Iterative Process

In order to initiate the process, any realistic ET_w schedule may be used. "Realistic" means a schedule that draws some positive response from the users. A schedule of queueing times which is so long that no jobs would be submitted is an unrealistic introductory schedule. The effect of assuming initially that the expected waiting time is zero for all values of T_s should be considered; it can be seen from the job value functions that, in order to maximize the net value, job a will be submitted at $T_s = 6$ (for which the net value is 100 value units), job c will be submitted at $T_s = 3$ (value = 80), and job d will be submitted at

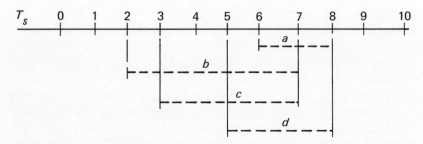

Figure 45 The processing times of jobs $a, b, c,$ and d and their times of submission T_s.

Table 18   Expected Waiting Time and Value of Job *a* for Different Submission Times

T_s^a	0	1	2	3	4	5	6	7	8	9	10	11	12	13	14	15	16
ET_w^a	0	0	0	4	7	6	8	7	6	5	4	3	2	1	0	0	0
V_a	40	50	60	50	27	39	20	29	37	42	43	42	37	29	20	10	0

T_s^a = submission time of job *a*.
ET_w^a = expected waiting time of job *a* for a given T_s^a.
V_a = value of job *a* for a given T_s^a.

$T_s = 5$ (value $= 140$). Job *b* can be submitted at any value of T_s, since its value is 120 whatever the time of submission. The arrival pattern and the length of each job, when a T_s of 2 for *b* is selected, are shown in Figure 45.

Subsequent Iterations

Actual ET_w schedules are now obtained for each job, assuming the other three jobs retain their initial submission times. For example, if job *a* is submitted at time zero, its queueing time is zero. This also holds for a T_s^a of one; however, at $T_s^a = 2$, job *b* also arrives. Since *a* is shorter than *b*, *a* would be run first, so the queueing time for *a* is still zero. At $T_s^a = 3$, the queueing time for *a* is 4, since *b* is already in service. The procedure is repeated, yielding the ET_w^a schedule shown in Table 18. Table 18 also indicates the value of job *a* at a different T_s^a, given the ET_w^a schedule.

It is clear that the initial T_s^a of 6 yields a net value of 20, whereas, if the submission times of the other jobs do not change, the best policy would be to submit job *a* at $T_s^a = 2$, to obtain the maximum net value of 60. When the procedure is repeated for all four jobs, the results summarized in Table 19 are obtained.

Users resubmit jobs *b*, *c*, and *d* as determined initially; however, job *a* is submitted at $T_s^a = 2$. Although under the initial configuration the total net value is 292 and the total computer running time is 14 units, resulting in a value per unit time of 20.8, the system is not in equilibrium.

For the next round of the iteration, the ET_w schedule of job *a* is retained, since the time of submission of job *a* is based on the submission pattern of Figure 45. The value schedule also is the same for job *a*; however, the shift in job *a* from $T_s^a = 6$ to $T_s^a = 2$ changes the ET_w and value schedules of the other three jobs. The procedure is

Table 19   First Iteration of Procedure

Job	Initial T_s	Value at Initial T_s	New Value	New T_s	Change?
a	6	20	60	2	Yes
b	2	120	120	2	No
c	3	60	60	3	No
d	5	92	92	5	No
Total		292	332		

repeated and an equilibrium solution is reached on the third iteration, as shown in Table 20.[1]

Jobs c and d do not change their times of submission in response to changes in the ET_w schedule, due to the stable nature of their value functions (especially job d, for which the value is positive only if it is submitted at $T_s = 5$). On the other hand, job b is very sensitive to the ET_w schedule. The equilibrium is reached when no further change in T_s for any job is indicated.

A Peak-Load Pricing Rule

Is this submission pattern system-optimal? Consider the following pricing rule:[2]

$$\text{Price} = 10, \text{ for } T_s = 1, 2, \text{ and } 0 > T_s \geq 12$$
$$\text{Price} = 0, \text{ otherwise.}$$

The only effect of the pricing rule is to induce job b to be submitted at $T_s^b = 0$ instead of $T_s^b = 1$. The system moves to a new equilibrium with a value of 24.2 value units per unit time. The pricing rule has the effect

---

[1] The equilibrium solution reached in Table 20 is far from the global optimum, as can be seen from the subsequent improvements in value achieved by implementing pricing and priority rules. In many cases, the equilibrium solution will depend on the initiation point of the process. The objective of the example is to demonstrate the iterative process rather than to achieve optimal solutions, for which techniques abound in the literature. See, for example, E. G. Coffman, Jr., ed., *Computer and Job-Shop Scheduling Theory*, New York, John Wiley and Sons, 1976.

[2] This rule would appear to contradict peak-load pricing rules.

Table 20 Summary of Results of Four Iterations

Iteration Number	Times of Submission				Value per Unit Time
	Job *a*	Job *b*	Job *c*	Job *d*	
0	6	2	3	5	20.8
1	2	2	3	5	20.6
2	2	1	3	5	22.6
3	3	1	3	5	23.7

of increasing the value of the system's objective function, indicating that the dynamic regulation resulting from the interaction between the ET_w schedule and the value functions does not in and of itself necessarily result in system optimization.

In the general nonlinear case, there is no assurance that a global optimum has been reached. The goal in this heuristic approach is to determine some "good" submission pattern and then to devise pricing and sequencing (priority) rules to effect the desired arrival pattern. The system was allowed to reach equilibrium through self-regulation, and then a peak-load price rule was introduced. If the price rule was introduced at the start of the iterative procedure, the same equilibrium would be reached. In general, this need not occur, and the equilibrium job sequence may be sensitive to the order in which the rules are applied.

A Priority Rule

Introducing the priority rule[3] that all other jobs should take priority over job *a* results in an equilibrium value per unit time of 24.1 units. This is close to, although less than, that obtained from the peak-load pricing rule.

Priority and Peak-Load Pricing Combination Rule

If the priority and peak-load pricing rules are combined, the process terminates in an equilibrium value per unit time of 25.6 units.

---

[3]In cases involving ties, preempting is not allowed.

Table 21 Summary of Results for Various Regulation Methods

Regulation Method	Equilibrium Value per Unit Time
Self-regulation	23.7
Peak-load pricing	24.2
Priority rule	24.1
Peak-load price and priority combined (1)	25.6
(2)	28.2

Thus the combination of rules, in this case, leads to a better solution than either rule used individually.

The "Best" Solution

If the peak-load pricing rule is changed to

Price = 0, for $T_s = 2$
Price = 5, otherwise,

a higher value per unit time of 28.2 units is obtained. Intuitively, this seems to be the global optimum for this particular system.

Note that this example has considered priority rules and peak-load pricing rules that are independent of the priorities. Priority-pricing rules, in which the higher priorities are available at higher prices, provide the organization with other means of control. Table 21 summarizes the results of this example.

AUTHOR INDEX

191

SUBJECT INDEX

Allocation of resources
  through pricing, 41
  see also Computer resource allocation
Applications programs, *see* Computer programs
Appointment systems
  cost of delay in, 108
  definition, 142–144
  in medical applications, 107
  in transportation, 107–108
Arrival densities
  high, 140–142
  low, 140–142, 144–145
Arrival rates
  effect on queueing time, 36
  random, 142–144, 173, 178
  variations in, 33
  see also Arrival densities
Automated evaluation system, 137
  job stream generator for, 138
  potential applications, 161–163
  reports from, 138

Backup computer systems, 69, 176
Balking, 4
Batch systems, 6
  environment, 165
  jobs in, 17

Billable charges, 23
Budgets
  allocation, 26, 29, 64, 79
  as a control, 37–40, 91
  definition, 21, 37
  effectiveness, 39
  internal, 32
  level, 37–39
  literature, 8–11
  marginal utility, 129
  organizational, 29
  period, 39
  perishability, 39–40
  for planning, 37
  transferability, 40
  see also Hard money; Restricted budgets; Soft money; Unrestricted budgets; User budgets
Budgeting, *see* Budgets

Capacity
  comparison of two systems, 173–176
  of data entry facility, 165
  definition, 20
  effect on processing time, 33
  of internal facility, 81, 90